# Christian Doctrine for Everyman:

## AN INTRODUCTION TO BAPTIST BELIEFS

## Jimmy A. Millikin

KRB Books
P.O. Box 143
Marion, Arkansas 72364

Scripture references and quotations,
unless otherwise stated, are from
the King James Version (AV)
of the Bible.

Library of Congress Card No. 78—104063

First Printing, 1976
Second Printing, 1979
Third Printing, 1989

Printed by
**⳨he King's**
**PRESS**
P.O. Box 144
Southaven, MS 38671

# FOREWORD

It is, indeed, a pleasure to introduce this theological handbook. These materials, first published in the **Arkansas Baptist Newsmagazine,** were so popular that Dr. Millikin was encouraged to have them printed in book form.

Though written for lay people, these articles contain a depth which will be helpful to preachers and experienced Bible teachers. The work combines simplicity of style, ease of writing, and clarity of spiritual truths.

Dr. Millikin is uniquely qualified both educationally and practically to produce a book of this type. He holds the Th.D. degree from Southwestern Baptist Theological Seminary, Fort Worth, Texas, with a major in New Testament. He has served churches in both rural and urban settings and his teaching experience has brought him in contact with a wide variety of people.

The author's deep love for the Bible is evident. Though one may occasionally differ with Dr. Millikin's interpretation of a particular doctrine, all will agree that he has made every effort to exalt the Word of God.

The book will serve Bible students in two ways. First, it provides a quick yet comprehensive overview of most Bible doctrines. Second, each teaching is documented with a wealth of scriptures to stimulate additional Bible study.

In dealing with each doctrine Dr. Millikin places Christ preeminent. His deep and abiding conviction should help combat many of the erroneous teachings of our time.

I sincerely commend this book to all who are committed to a better understanding of God's truth.

J. Everett Sneed, Editor
**Arkansas Baptist Newsmagazine**

# PREFACE

These doctrinal studies first appeared in the **Arkansas Baptist Newsmagazine** in a weekly column called "Doctrines of the Faith." They were written in response to a request by Dr. Charles Ashcraft, Executive Secretary of the Arkansas Baptist Convention, to contribute to the column. The articles appear here essentially unchanged.

The reader should keep in mind that the articles were originally written with the general reading public in mind. They were aimed at people who are not trained theologians nor skilled Bible scholars. My purpose was to communicate Christian truth in a clear understandable fashion to the average person in the pew. Indeed, it seems to me that this should be the ultimate goal of every professional theologian and Bible scholar. I have felt for some time that too many theological treatises were written only for the benefit of other theologians.

No originality is claimed in the presentation of these studies. The theological specialist who may happen to peruse this volume looking for new light or a fresh approach to old truths will no doubt be disappointed. My approach has been from the standpoint of a conventional systematic treatment. The ideas presented here may fairly be considered orthodox and traditional. I make no apology for this. It just may be, in light of the widespread neglect of the old truths, that this fact may contribute to the novelty of this work.

I am gratified to know that to some extent my purpose in writing the original articles was accomplished. Numerous lay people in the churches of Arkansas have told me through both oral and written communication of the helpfulness of the studies. Many pastors have also related to me their appreciation for the articles. I am told that many of the articles formed the basis of sermons. It is because of the encouragement of these people that I have ventured to submit the articles for publication.

I expect any author is indebted to others for his work. This is certainly true of this writer. I wish to acknowledge my indebtedness to Dr. Charles Ashcraft who invited and challenged me to write the studies in the first place, and gave me many words of encouragement while writing them. Also I want to thank Dr. Everett Sneed who became editor of the **Arkansas Baptist Newsmagazine** after I began the series and asked me to continue with the column. Most of all I want to express my appreciation to Arkansas Baptists whose words of appreciation inspired me to meet weekly deadlines. I owe a great deal to Arkansas Baptists for what I am and for whatever good I may become in the Lord's work. It is to these dear people I wish to dedicate this volume on Christian doctrine.

# TABLE OF CONTENTS

# INTRODUCTION: THE

# NEED FOR DOCTRINE

Anyone who attempts to write on doctrinal matters in our day feels almost obliged to justify the need. The spirit of this modern age, both inside and outside religious circles, is decidedly against the setting forth of definite doctrines in any realm. Many Christian people are impatient with and even suspicious of doctrine. The very word conjures up all kinds of evil associations in the minds of some - - narrow-mindedness, bigotry, intolerance, and divisiveness, to name a few.

Many factors in contemporary society have contributed to this attitude. The ecumenical movement has minimized doctrinal distictiveness for years for the sake of unity. Modern education has indoctrinated several generations of students against all forms of indoctrination. In the academic realm there is a widespread feeling that all truth is relative, that nothing can be known for sure, especially religious truth. There is a general revolt against any authoritarian approach to truth and life. All these factors, along with others, have helped to create an anti-doctrinal climate in our churches today.

A growing number of religious leaders support the anti-doctrinal spirit of today. They deny the need for setting forth any definite doctrines of the Christian faith. Christianity, it is claimed, is primarily a matter of experience or feeling, good will, and practical social activity. The doctrinal aspects are non-essential, and may even be a hindrance.

We acknowledge, of course, that experience, good will, and practical social activity are vital elements of the Christian faith. However, we maintain that doctrines are also essential. There are others, but we give only four reasons why Christian doctrine is necessary.

11

First, the New Testament plainly indicates that there is a doctrinal element in Christianity. The Scriptures are profitable for doctrine (2 Tim. 3:16). The early believers continued steadfastly in the apostles' doctrine (Acts 2:42), and filled Jerusalem with that doctrine (Acts 5:28). Christian workers are urged to give attendance to doctrine (I Tim. 4:13, 16), and those who do are to be given special honor (I Tim. 5:17).

In the New Testament there is such a thing as sound doctrine (I Tim. 1:10; 4:6; 2 Tim. 4:3; Tit. 1: 9; 2:11), and this doctrine is clearly recognizable (2 Tim. 3:10). Believers are frequently warned against false doctrine (Eph. 4:14; Rom. 16:17; Heb. 13:9), and there are serious consequences of not abiding in the doctrine of Christ (2 Jn. 9, 10). A rejection of the doctrinal element in Christianity really amounts to a rejection of the New Testament witness.

Second, doctrine is necessary in order to communicate the Christian faith. Christians are called upon to be witnesses, not merely to an inner experience, but to the whole truth about Jesus Christ and His redemption for men (Acts 20:20, 27; Eph. 4:14). As a witness it is important that the Christian believer know and tell the truth, the whole truth, and nothing but the truth. It thus makes a big difference what our doctrines are and that we know what they are.

Third, Christian doctrine is necessary in order to defend the Christian faith. It is common today to assert that the gospel needs no defending, it only needs preaching. There is a great deal of truth in this, but it is not the whole truth. Neither is it in agreement with the teaching and example of the New Testament.

Paul was set for the defense of the gospel (Phil. 1:17). The Christian is exhorted to contend for the faith. (Phil. 1:27; Jude 3). Believers are enjoined to "know how to answer every man" (Col. 4:6), and to "be able to give an answer of the hope" that is in them (I Pet. 3:15). In order to do this we must know what the "faith" is.

Finally, doctrine is necessary in order to preserve the faith. Paul exhorts Timothy to be faithful to the things he had been taught and in turn to commit them to others who would be faithful (2 Tim. 2:2). The obvious concern of Paul here is the faithful preservation of the faith.

There is a faith "once delivered to the saints" (Jude 3). The apostles were true to this faith and faithful in transmitting it to the next generation. Many generations since have been true to this faith. It has finally reached us. Now we are to be true to its teachings and faithfully pass it on to the next generation. The need to know and understand the doctrines of the faith is still an imperative for our day.

# PART I

## THE BIBLE AND REVELATION

# 1. THE BIBLE—OUR AUTHORITY FOR DOCTRINE

Where do we get our authority for the doctrines we believe and teach? By what authority do we accept some doctrines and reject others? Are doctrinal beliefs simply a matter of personal opinion? Or is there some standard by which all doctrinal beliefs may be judged?

The Baptist answer to these crucial questions concerning religious authority is that there is one final authoritative source for Christian doctrine. The introduction to the **Baptist Faith and Message** adopted by the Southern Baptist Convention in 1963 states that "the sole authority for faith and practice among Baptists is the Scriptures of the Old and New Testaments." This is no recent statement by Baptists. It is an ancient premise found in the oldest Baptist statements of faith.

The principle of "sole authroity" needs special emphasis here. The Baptist position recognizes the Bible as the only final authority for doctrinal beliefs for Christians. This means that the Scriptures are to be put above all other claims for doctrinal authority -- religious experience, individual conscience, human reason, church traditions, or whatever.

The question may properly be asked, "Why do we accept the Bible and the Bible only as the final authority?" Is this not in itself a mere opinion or assumption? For the Christian it is not. Our acceptance of the sole authority of the Bible is based on solid factual evidence.

The evidence for our view of the Bible is Jesus himself. The attitude of Jesus toward the Scriptures is not a matter of opinion. It is a matter of factual record for any and all to examine. This record reveals that Jesus accepted the absolute authority of the Scriptures.

Jesus was concerned that his attitude toward Scripture not be misunderstood, and thus stated plainly that he did not come to set aside Scripture but to confirm its abiding authority (Mt. 5:17). He did not hesitate to equate Scripture with the words of God (Mt. 15:4; 19: 4-6). He often answered questions, justified his actions, and settled doctrinal issues with a simple, "It stands written" (Mt. 4:4; Mk. 9:12; 11:17; Jn. 6:45), or "have you not read?" (Mt. 19:4; 21:16; Lk. 4:21). For Jesus, if a matter is written in Scripture then it is settled. There can be no appeal against Scripture, for it has legal, binding force, and its authority cannot be broken (Jn. 10:35).

Furthermore, Jesus willingly submitted himself to the authority of Scripture. There were things he **must** do because they were written in the Scriptures of him (Mk. 8:31; 14:21; Lk. 2:49; 18:31). He met Satan with the declared intention of obeying the Scriptures (Mt. 4:4ff.). He interpreted his mission in the light of the Old Testament prophecies (Lk. 13:31; 24:44). He finally committed himself to die in obedience to the Scriptures (Mt. 26:53f.).

The chief reason, then, why we accept the sole authority of the Bible is because Christ did. There are other reasons, such as the testimony of the apostles and the witness of the Bible to its own authority. However, the main reason is because of Christ. Christ is our Lord, and he has taught us by word and example that the Scriptures have divine authority.

## 2. THE INSPIRATION OF THE BIBLE: ITS DIVINE ORIGIN

The inspiration of the Bible is a fundamental and most important doctrine of the Christian faith. The first article in the **Baptist Faith and Message** deals with the doctrine of Scripture and appropriately opens with the statement: "The Bible was written by men divinely inspired. . ." Baptists thus believe in the divine inspiration of the Bible.

Since the word "inspired" is used in so many ways today, there is need to explain what is meant when we say the Bible is inspired. For example, we commonly use the word "inspired" to refer to a feeling or a heightening of one's natural ability, as when we say Shakespeare was inspired to write great plays or Fanny Crosby was inspired to write great hymns. The inspiration of the Bible must not be confused with this common usage of the word today.

With reference to the Bible the word "inspired" has a unique and quite different meaning. Basically, it affirms two things about the Bible: (1) its divine origin and (2) its supernatural nature. Here we will consider the divine origin and discuss its supernatural nature in the next study.

To say the Bible is divinely inspired means that the Bible has a divine origin. The key biblical passage from which we get our doctrine of inspiration is 2 Tim. 3:16. There we read: "All Scripture is given by inspiration of God." Actually the six English words, "is given by inspiration of God," is a translation of only one Greek word. The word is **theopneustos** and means "God-breathed," or "breathed out by God."

The breath of God is often associated in the Old Testament with the creative activity of God. The Lord "breathed" into man the

15

"breath of life" and he "became a living soul" (Gen. 2:7). "By the word of the Lord were the heavens made; and all the host of them by the breath of his mouth" (Psa. 33:6). The term "God-breathed" was one of the clearest and strongest terms Paul could have used to affirm the divine origin of Scripture.

The divine origin of Scripture is also emphasized in 2 Peter 1:20f. Here it is stated that no prophecy of Scripture ever came "by the will of man," but "holy men of God spake as they were moved by the Holy Ghost." That is, Scripture did not originate in the genius of man, nor is it the result of human research. It has a divine origin.

There are a number of other references in the Bible which indicate the supernatural origin of Scripture. The idea of men moved by the Spirit and compelled to speak God's word is found throughout the Old Testament (cf. Ex. 4:10-16; 7:1; 2 Sam. 23:2; Mic. 3:8; Zec. 7:12). The phrases "the Lord spake," "the word of the Lord came," are used over 3,000 times in the Old Testament. The meaning is clear. The men of the Old Testament did not speak or write as a result of their own insights. Their words originated with God.

To say the Bible has a divine origin in no way denies that men were involved in its writing. Neither does it imply that the human writers of the Bible were mere writing machines. It simply means that the Holy Spirit worked through human instrumentality in such a way that it resulted in producing what God wanted written. Even though human instrumentality was used, as the **Baptist Faith and Message** puts it, the Bible "has God for its author."


### 3. THE INSPIRATION OF THE BIBLE:
### ITS SUPERNATURAL NATURE

"All Scripture is given by inspiration of God" (2 Tim. 3:16). In the previous study it was indicated that this statement affirms at least two things about the Bible: (1) its divine origin and (2) its supernatural nature. It was previously pointed out that the phrase "given by inspiration of God" in 2 Tim. 3:16 is a translation of the Greek word, **theopneustos,** and means "God-breathed." The emphasis is that Scripture **itself** is inspired or rather breathed out by God. This verse says nothing about the inner experiences of the human authors of the Bible. Its meaning is that Scripture is a divine utterance of God; it is a product of God's activity and consequently possesses a unique divine quality.

#### God's Word
To say the Bible has a unique divine quality has several important

implications. In the first place, it means that **it is God's Word.** It does not simply contain the Word of God, nor is it a mere witness to the Word of God. The Bible is in and of itself the written Word of God. The words of Scripture are breathed out by God and are themselves divine utterances.

That this is the biblical doctrine of Scripture is clear. Though modern theologians generally will not identify Holy Scripture with the Word of God, the Bible itself is not afraid to do so. The prophets repeatedly identified their prophecies with the Word of God by a "thus saith the Lord" and similar expressions (Jer. 11:1,2; Isa. 1:1, 10). The Old Testament is always cited in the New Testament as the speaking of God (cf. Mt. 1:22; Acts 28:25). Jesus himself, expressly equates the Word of God with Scripture (Jn. 10:35).

In a number of passages the Scriptures and God are so closely connected that the two are indistinguishable. For example, sometimes the Scriptures are spoken of as if they were God (cf. Gen. 12: 1-3 with Gal. 3:8; and Ex. 9:16 with Rom. 9:17). In other passages God is spoken of as if He were the Scriptures (cf. Gen. 2:24 with Mt. 19: 4-5). These and other passages demonstrate that the writers of the New Testament made an absolute identification of Scripture with the speaking of God. The Scriptural approach to Scripture is thus to regard it as the Word of God.

### Infallible and Inerrant

To say the Bible has a divine nature, in the second place, means that **it possesses the qualities of infallibility and inerrancy.** This simply means that the Bible does not deceive or mislead. It contains no falsehoods nor contradictions. There is nothing in the Scriptures which is unworthy of an infallible God who cannot lie.

Belief in the infallibility and inerrancy of the Bible has been a common belief of Christians since the time of the Apostles. The great majority of Evangelicals are still accustomed to speaking of the Bible as infallible and inerrant today. It is an ancient Baptist belief and is expressed in the **Baptist Faith and Message** adopted by the SBC in 1963. It says of the Bible: "It has ... truth, without any mixture of error, for its matter."

Contrary to the thinking of many today, it does make a difference as to whether one does or does not accept the infallibility and inerrancy of the Bible. These two qualities are necessary properties of God's Word. If the Bible contains errors and falsehoods then it cannot be God's Word, for God cannot lie (Tit. 1:2). On the other hand, if one believes the Bible in its entirety is the Word of God, he will have no trouble in believing it to be infallible and inerrant.

17

**Divine Authority**

In the third place, the unique Divinity of the Bible means it has divine authority. It is authoritative both in the area of doctrine and in the area of conduct. Whatever the Bible teaches as true, the Christian is to believe, regardless of the consensus of modern thought. However the Bible teaches us to live, we are to obey, regardless of what new "life styles" the majority of the now generation may adopt.

In summary, to say the Bible is divine in its nature means that whatever the Bible says, God says.

## 4. THE DOCTRINE OF REVELATION: INTRODUCTION

How is God known? This is perhaps the most basic question in any religious system. Its answer forms the foundation for all the other teachings of a religion. It is a question which is at the very heart of the Bible and Christianity.

The Christian doctrine which deals with the question of man's knowledge of God is called revelation. Somehow the term "revelation" has not left the impression on many Baptists as referring to a doctrine of the Christian faith. At least it seems that way to me. I can remember the time when the only association I made with the word was that it was the title of the last book of the Bible. Even the **Baptist Faith and Message** does not contain a separate article on this doctrine.

A good place to begin, therefore, in discussing revelation is with a definition of the doctrine. The word "revelation" means an "uncovering," a "disclosure", an "unveiling". Thus, in Christian doctrine it has to do with the disclosure or manifestation of God and His will to His creatures. In other words, the doctrine of revelation seeks to answer the question, "How is God known?"

In order to bring the Christian answer into clearer focus, it may be helpful to point out that basically there are two views as to how God is know by man. One view says that man **discovers** God. This view is sometimes called **natural religion** or **natural theology..**

The discovery approach to a knowledge of God is basically anti-supernaturalistic in its outlook. It denies that there has been or could ever be anything like a supernatural self-revelation of God. Everything that can be known about God, His existence and His attributes, must be apprehended in nature or natural phenomena by man's own mind. What man knows of God he has found through a progressive discovery of truth.

18

The other view of man's knowledge of God holds that God is revealed to man. This view is sometimes called revealed religion or theism. In the thought of theism God is an immortal and infinite Being, while man is a mortal and finite creature. God is consequently altogether beyond man. Therefore, man's mind, no matter how wonderful and effective it may be in other areas, cannot climb up to the infinite mind of God (cf. Isa. 55: 8-9). Thus, left to himself, man would never discover God as he really is. A true, authoritative and sufficient knowledge of God is possible only by means of a supernatural self-disclosure of God Himself.

It should be evident that the Christian religion lays claim to being a revealed religion. The Christian teaching about God is not a product of man's search after God, but has been distinctly revealed by God. The Christian religion is quite frankly based on a supernatural revelation by God (Mt. 16:17; Eph. 3:5).

The Christian claim is that God has taken the initiative to reveal Himself. He has done this in two ways. First, He has revealed Himself through His mighty deeds (Psa. 78:4; Jn. 20: 30-31). Second, He has revealed His truth and will through His words (Heb. 1:1; Amos 3:8). God has acted and God has spoken. Through the one He has revealed His person. Through the other He has revealed His truth about Himself and His purpose.

How then does man know God? It is not through human discovery but through divine revelation. It is not through the wisdom of man but through the Word of God (Isa. 55: 8-14; I Cor. 1: 16-31).


## 5. GOD REVEALED IN NATURE

The doctrine of revelation is commonly divided into two areas -- general revelation and special revelation. General revelation is that revelation which God makes to all men. It is sometimes called natural revelation because it is communicated through the means of natural phenomena.

By contrast, special revelation is that revelation which relates specifically to God's program of redemption. It is not given to all men but to a particular chosen people, to Israel in the Old Testament and to Christ's church in the New Testament. This revelation is sometimes called supernatural revelation because it is made through the supernatural intervention of God in the natural course of things.

Our concern in this study is with the general revelation of God. The Biblical teaching on this aspect of God's revelation may be summarized as follows:

First, the general revelation of God is made to man through natural phenomena apart from the Bible. This natural phenomena consists primarily of two elements -- the universe (nature proper) and man's conscience. That is, God has revealed Himself through the wonders of the world without man (Psa. 19: 1-6; Rom. 1:20), and through the moral law which God has put within man (Rom. 2: 14-16).

Second, this general revelation in natural phenomena is a genuine revelation of God. There is sufficient evidence in nature to demonstrate that something beyond nature exists, that this something is the personal God, that this God is allwise, powerful, and good (Mt. 6: 24-34; Acts 14: 17; 17: 26-29; Rom. 1:20). Furthermore, through the moral law in man (conscience) God is revealed as a righteous God who demands righteousness of man (Rom. 2: 14-16).

The point needing emphasis here is that, from the biblical viewpoint, the evidences for God in natural phenomena are so valid that man can be justly condemned even though he has never heard the gospel. He ought to discern God in the world without and in his conscience within, and if he does not, it is because he will not (Rom. 1: 19-32).

Third, the general revelation of God is made to all people. There is, therefore, a sense in which every person has some knowledge of God. God has not left Himself "without witness" in any part of the earth (Acts 14:17). "There is no speech nor language" where the divine voice in nature cannot be heard (Psa. 19: 3).

Fourth, and very important, the general revelation of God in natural phenomena is inadequate to meet the spiritual needs of man. It is inadequate for two reasons:

One reason is because sin has blinded man so that he fails to see God clearly in His general revelation. God is truly revealed and man ought to be able to see and know God through this revelation. However, sin causes man to pervert and distort this revelation (Rom. 1: 22-25), and to willfully reject the God who is revealed (Rom. 1: 28).

A second reason is because general revelation does not reveal the grace of God. God's existence, power, wisdom, and even His goodness may be seen in His general revelation. However, man is a sinner and is separated from God. He needs to have his sins forgiven and enter into a personal relationship with God. This he cannot do for himself. This is possible only through the manifestation of God's grace. And this in turn necessitates a "special" or "supernatural" revelation.

## 6. GOD'S "SPECIAL" REVELATION

Man can know God only because God has taken the initiative to reveal Himself. Left to himself man would never find God. Man cannot see (Jn. 1: 18), nor approach (I Tim. 6: 16), nor search out (Job 11: 7; Isa. 55:8) God with his own unaided abilities. Man cannot know God unless He acts to make Himself known. This God has done. We call this revelation.

We have seen that a part of God's revelation is in natural phenomena. This is known as "general" revelation. We have also observed that this "general" revelation in nature is inadequate to meet the spiritual needs of man. This makes necessary a "special" revelation. The general features of this "special" revelation may be outlined as follows:

### The Record

First, the record of God's "special" revelation is the Bible. While the Bible acknowledges the existence and validity of a "general" revelation in nature, its emphasis centers on "special" revelation. In fact, "special" revelation is so inseparable from the Bible that it is often called "biblical" revelation. The Christian thus has two records of God's total revelatory work--nature which contains His general revelation, and the Bible which contains His special revelation.

### The Means

Second, God's "special" revelation is made known through supernatural means. By this we mean that God makes Himself known through a supernatural intervention in the natural course of things. God breaks through, so to speak, in extraordinary ways into into the ordinary events of history and nature.

The supernatural means through which God reveals Himself in "special" revelation may be grouped under two major heads: (1) divine (miraculous) acts in human history and (2) divine (supernaturally given) words of truth. To put it another way, God has acted supernaturally before the eyes of man (Jn. 1: 14), and He has spoken supernaturally to the ears and mind of man (Heb. 1:1).

### The Necessity

Third, the "special" revelation of God was made necessary because of sin. Sin has affected man in two important ways. One, his eyes have been blinded to the extent that he is unable to see God clearly in nature (Acts 17: 23; Eph. 4: 17-19). Not only is man unable to see God clearly but he willfully distorts what he is able to perceive (Rom. 1: 22-25).

The second effect is that sin has brought guilt and condemnation upon man (Rom. 3: 19) and has separated him from God (Eph. 2: 12). If man is to be forgiven and his fellowship with God restored, then God must act in some special supernatural way to do it. This He has done in 'special' revelation (Rom. 1: 16-17; Jn. 1: 18).

### The Purpose
Fourth, the primary purpose of "special" revelation is the salvation of men. Its design is to rescue broken and deformed sinners from their sin and its consequences. Just as sin has blinded man's eyes to God and broken his fellowship with God, so "special" revelation has the purpose of giving man a true knowledge of God (Col. 3: 10) and restoring his fellowship with Him (II Cor. 5: 18-21; Eph. 2: 12-22).

# PART II

## THE DOCTRINE OF GOD

# 7. THE NATURE OF GOD

In the last several studies we have been emphasizing that God has taken the initiative to reveal Himself to man. He has done this in several ways. He has acted in history, and He has spoken His word to men. Now we turn to the question, "What kind of God has He revealed Himself to be?"

The importance of this question in any system of religious thought cannot be overemphasized. One's idea of God will largely determine all his other religious beliefs. What a person believes about man, salvation, the future -- these and almost every other imaginable religious concern--will depend on what he thinks about God.

The doctrine of God is a very broad area of Christian turth. Indeed, God is the central subject matter of the entire Bible. God has displayed His character and attributes on every page of Holy Scripture. Our concern here will be with only the aspect of His nature. Who is this God Who has shown Himself to man? What kind of Being is He? What is His essential nature?

## Unity

First, **God is one.** As the **Baptist Faith and Message** puts it, "There is one and only one living and true God" (Art. II). This belief is known as monotheism. No other truth about God in the Bible, especially in the Old Testament, receives more emphasis than this fact. The first and chief commandment is a command to monotheism (Ex. 20: 3). Assent and obedience to this command forms the basic duty of life (Deut. 6:4; Mk. 12: 28-30).

## Spirituality

Second, **God is a spiritual Being.** The very essence of God's being is Spriit (Jn. 4:24). That is, God has no material element in His essential nature. He does not have a body (Isa. 31:3).

As pure Spirit God is invisible (Rom. 1:20; I Tim. 1:17), and no likeness can be formed of Him (Deut. 4: 15-23; Isa. 40: 25), nor can He be apprehended by physical means (Jn. 4: 24; Acts 17: 25). Since God is Spirit He cannot be limited by space, nor can He be confined to any one place (I Kgs. 8:27; Acts 7: 48; 17: 24). No one can escape His presence, for He is everywhere (Psa. 139: 7-10; Acts 17: 27-28).

## Personal

Third, **God is a personal Being.** God is no mere impersonal intelligent principle, as some so-called "sophisticated" views of God would have us believe. God has revealed Himself as "I" and speaks to man as "you." He has a personal name (Ex. 3: 14; 6: 1-3).

God possesses all the essential qualities of personality -- He thinks (Psa. 92: 5; Isa. 55: 8f.); He wills (Psa. 115: 3; Dan. 4: 35; Eph. 1:5); He feels (Psa. 103: 13; Jn. 3:16); He acts (Gen. 1:1). Above all, God is revealed as personal in His Son who has shown us that man can have a personal relationship with God and call Him "Father" (Mt. 6:9).

### Triune

Fourth, **God is tri-personal.** "The eternal God reveals Himself to us as Father, Son, and Holy Spirit, with distinct personal attributes, but without division of nature, essence, or being" (**Baptist Faith and Message,** Art. II). That is, God is one but He is also triune or trinity. This is a difficult concept, but it is at the very heart of the New Testament revelation of God. God's New Testament name is Father, Son, and Holy Spirit (Mt. 28: 19; cf. II Cor. 13: 14; I Pe. 1:2).

## 8. THE ATTRIBUTES OF GOD

God has not only revealed that He **is**; He has also told us **something** about Himself. In an old Baptist catechism there is a question which asks, "What is God?" It answers: "God is Spirit, infinite, eternal, and unchangeable in His being, wisdom, power, holiness, justice, goodness, and truth" (**Spurgeon's Catechism,** Question 4).

### Meaning

Our more recent **Baptist Faith and Message** makes a similar attempt at describing God when it states: "God is infinite in holiness and all other perfections" (Art. II). And again: "He is all powerful, all loving, and all wise" (Art. II, A).

Most of the terms used in the above descriptions of God are called attributes. An attribute is a quality or characteristic of a thing or person. Thus, the attributes of God are those distinguishing qualities which mark or characterize God. In other words, the attributes of God describe what God is like.

Any discussion of what God is like must acknowledge that there is a certain incomprehensibility about God. We are dealing here with a deep and unspeakable mystery. Our minds are not great enough to take in so great a thought, nor is human language adequate to describe completely what God is like.

On the other hand, God has been pleased to tell us something about Himself. It is God Himself who reveals His attributes to us in

Scripture. Hence we may be sure that the attributes ascribed to God in the Bible are real and that they describe God as He really is.

The attributes which are ascribed to God in the Scriptures are many. He is infinite (Job 11:7), eternal (Psa. 90: 2), unchangeable (Ja. 1: 17), all wise (Psa. 147: 5), all powerful (Mt. 19: 26), holy (Rev. 4:8), just (Isa. 45: 21), merciful, good, and true (Ex. 34: 6f.). These and a number of other terms are used to describe in some sense what God is like.

## Classification

Because of the great number of attributes which may be ascribed to God, attempts have been made in doctrinal studies to classify them into various groups. It is common, for example, to call some the **communicable** attributes and others the **incommunicable** attributes. The **communicable** attributes are those which, to a limited degree, may be shared by man. The **incommunicable** attributes are those which belong only to God and cannot be shared by any of His creatures.

Some theologians are not pleased with the above classification and prefer other groupings. Others feel that all attempts to divide the attributes are useless. It seems, however, that some division is helpful. Four our purpose here, therefore, we will divide the attributes of God into the following two areas:

First, some of the attributes describe God as an absolute Being. By "absolute" we mean that God is self-existent, perfect and unlimited in His Being, that He is not dependent on anything outside Himself. Such terms as all-powerful, all-wise, infinite, and perfect describe God as absolute.

Second, other attributes describe God as a **moral** Being. God has revealed Himself as one supremely concerned about right and wrong. Such terms as holiness, righteousness, goodness, truth, love, tell us of God's moral nature and that His dealings with men must be understood in moral terms.

It is with these two aspects of God that we will be concerned in the next two studies.

## 9. THE HOLINESS OF GOD

God has revealed Himself to be a moral being. This means that God distinguishes between right and wrong, and that He is very much concerned about what is right.

Many terms have been used to describe the moral nature of God: such as holiness, righteousness, justice, truthfulness, mercy, love, wrath, grace, and others. It would be instructive to discuss each of these terms separately. However, the nature of these studies will not permit such a detailed treatment. Besides, some of the terms convey similar ideas. Thus, to save space and repetition we will discuss the moral nature of God under one basis concept—His holiness.

The origin of the term "holy" is not clear. Its basic meaning seems to be that of separateness or apartness. Thus, God's holiness means that He is separate and different from things created. He is infinitely exalted above His creation. In this sense, holiness is not a particular and distinct attribute of God at all. It is a description of all that God is and does. Holiness is the very essence of God's being. It is God Himself.

In a true sense, however, holiness may be seen as a particular attribute. As such it describes God in two respects. Negatively, it means that God is free from all that is impure (Hab. 1: 13). Positively, it denotes that God embodies all that is pure and good. The apostle John states both of these aspects when he declares: "God is light, and in him is no darkness at all" (I John 1:5).

If there is any difference in importance in the attributes of God, His holiness would certainly occupy the first place. The term "holy" is used more frequently in the Bible than any other to describe God. Whenever God made Himself known through visions or personal appearances, the thing that stood out the most was His holiness (cf. Ex. 3: 1-6; Isa. 6: 1-8; Rev. 4:8). The prophet Isaiah alone speaks of God as the "Holy One" some thirty times.

Hence, there is a biblical basis for considering holiness to be the fundamental attribute of God, the governing quality in His nature. From God's holiness issues all of His other moral attributes. Actually, the other attributes may be looked upon as manifestations of God's holiness.

God's holiness, for example, is manifested in His concern with right and wrong; that is God is **righteous** and **just** in his dealings with men. He is a God of **truth**. Because he is righteous God hates sin and condemns it in man; hence, God has the quality of **wrath** (Psa. 11: 4-7; Rom. 1: 18).

Also, because God is holy, He is **good**. God's goodness in turn is manifested in His **mercy, grace,** and **longsuffering** (Ex. 33:19; 34: 6-7). The much emphasized attribute of **love** in the New Testament is simply God's holiness manifested in its compassionate goodness. This is the thing that makes God's love so unbelievable and astonishing; it is the love of the Holy One (Isa. 52: 8-10).

The holiness of God, then, is the sum total of all God's moral attributes. Holiness is His name (Isa. 57: 15). It is synonymous with deity. It is the one attribute by which God wishes to be remembered (Psa. 30: 4; 97: 12). It is the attribute which exalts and glorifies God the most (Psa. 99).

Let us keep this fact in mind as we continue these doctrinal studies. In this day of permissiveness which tends to deny the awfulness of sin, we need a new vision of God's holiness. Our view of the necessity of Christ's death for sin will largely depend on our view of God's holiness. Light views of sin and the atonement will result from a light view of God's holiness.

## 10. THE ABSOLUTENESS OF GOD

The absoluteness of God is not an easy concept for us to grasp. This is due, no doubt, to the fact that we are finite creatures. As fallen creatures, we have never achieved or experienced absoluteness in any form. Thus it is difficult for us to understand God's absoluteness. Nevertheless, the term "absoluteness" denotes an idea that we cannot do away with in our concept of God. Basically, it conveys two essential characteristics of God's nature.

### Self-existence

First, it denotes that God is an independent, self-existent Being. God was not caused, nor is He dependent on anything outside Himself for His existence. He revealed Himself to Moses as "I am that I am" (Ex. 3: 14). He is not dependent on the world for life and being; He does not need anything (Acts 17:25). He is the living God who "has life in Himself" (Jn. 5:26). In other words, God has the source and ground of His being in Himself.

While God is not dependent on anything outside Himself for His existence, everything else is dependent on God for its existence. God is the source of all that lives and exists. God existed before the world began and He can exist without the world, but the world and man cannot exist without God (Acts 17: 25).

To be sure, this is hard to understand. It involves the proverbial question, "Where did God come from?" The only answer is that God always was. He has no beginning. He is the uncaused Cause. Incomprehensible but true!

### Unlimited

The second idea the absoluteness of God denotes is that God is unlimited in His Being. Another term sometimes used to express this idea is "infinity." We often say that God is infinite and man is finite. By this we mean that God is perfect and unlimited, whereas man is imperfect and limited.

God is perfect and unlimited in every respect in which we can think of Him. However, there are four particular areas which are usually emphasized:

First, **God is unlimited by time.** This is usually expressed by the term "eternal." When we say God is eternal we mean that He has neither beginning nor end (Rev. 1: 8). God does not grow, develop, and become old (Psa. 102: 24-27; Mal. 3:6). He existed before the world began, and He will continue when history has ended.

Second, **God is unlimited by space.** This concept is expressed by the term "omnipresence." God is everywhere. He fills the whole heaven and earth (Jer. 23: 23f.). He is "not far from every one of us; for in Him we live, and move, and have our being" (Acts 17: 27f.). No one can escape this allpresent God (Psa. 139).

Third, **God is unlimited in His knowledge.** This we call "omniscience." God knows everything. His knowledge is not limited by time, by the amount of knowledge in the world, nor anything else. "His understanding is infinite" (Psa. 147: 5). He knows the future and the past as well as the present. He knows even the smallest details, like the numbering of the hairs of our heads (Lk. 12: 7).

Fourth, **God is unlimited in His power.** This is known as "omnipotence." It means that God's power knows no bounds or limitations. God can do anything He wills to do. He has power over the world of nature (Psa. 107: 25-29), heavenly creatures (Dan. 4; 35), and human actions (Ja. 4: 12-15). Even Satan is under the power and authority of God (Jb. 1: 12; Lk. 22: 31-32). Nothing is too hard for God (Gen. 18:14). With Him all things are possible (Mt. 19: 26).

Some modern views of God hold to a limited, finite God who is simply doing the best He can to overcome sin and evil. According to these views even God cannot guarantee the outcome. This is not the God of the Bible. The God of the Bible is an absolutist God who has all authority and power. He has things under His control. He knows the outcome, and it will be according to His divine purpose (Eph. 1: 11). Hallelujah!

## 11. THE DOCTRINE OF THE TRINITY

Any way you look at it, the doctrine of the Trinity is a deep mystery which cannot be fathomed completely by the finite mind. There is no way to adequately explain it to satisfy man's intellect. It defies logic and ordinary arithmetic. We can only say with another, "Off with our shoes, please, for the Holy Trinity is the holy ground."

The difficulty of explaining and understanding the Trinity has caused it to be ridiculed by unbelievers and neglected by believers. It is very rarely the topic of a sermon. It is seldom discussed in Bible classes. As a result many Christians have never heard of the term "trinity," and even more do not know what it means.

## Meaning

By the Trinity Christians mean that God is three persons existing in a single, undivided nature. **The Baptist Faith and Message** states it thus: "The eternal God reveals Himself to us as Father, Son, and Holy Spirit, with distinct personal attributes, but without division of nature, essence, or being." In other words, the one God is three-personed.

While the Trinity is admittedly difficult, there can be no reasonable doubt that it is taught in the Bible. It is intimated in the Old Testament and clearly taught in the New Testament. For this reason Christians have insisted that the doctrine is to be believed even though it cannot be completely understood.

## Old Testament Background

There are four facts in the Old Testament which clearly intimate that God has a plural personality. (1) One of the most common names for God is a plural name (Elohim). (2) God is referred to with a plural personal pronoun (Gen. 1:26; 11:7; Isa. 6:8). (3) The "angel of the Lord" is often spoken of in such a way as to suggest he is God and yet distinct from him (see esp. Gen. 16:7-14; and Gen. 18-19). (4) The divine Spirit is described as one with God and yet is distinguished from him (Gen. 1:2; Jgs. 6:34; Psa. 139:7-10).

## New Testament Teaching

Where the Trinity is implied in the Old Testament, it is clearly taught in the New Testament. It is true that the word "trinity" is not found in the New Testament, yet the idea is clearly there. "Trinity" is only a term which is used to describe the facts revealed.

There are three facts in the New Testament which demand the formation of the doctrine of the Trinity. (1) The New Testament clearly teaches that there is only one God (Jn. 17:3; I Cor. 8:6; Eph. 4:6). (2) The New Testament explicitly states that Jesus is God, yet distinct from the Father (Jn. 1:1; 20:28; I Tim. 3:16). (3) The Divine Spirit is revealed as a distinct personality (Jn. 14-16). Any Christian view of God must harmonize all of these facts. The doctrine of the Trinity is an attempt to do this.

## Doctrinal Explanation

In stating the Christian doctrine of the Trinity, two essential facts must be emphasized. First, the three "persons" of the one Godhead must be differentiated. God must not be seen as merely manifesting himself sometimes as Father, sometimes as Son, and sometimes as Holy Spirit. Father, Son, and Holy Spirit all exist at the same time with "distinct personal attributes" and enjoy a personal relation with each other (cf. Jn. 1: 29-34; Mt. 28: 19; II Cor. 13: 14; Jn. 14-16; Eph. 2: 18; I Pet. 1: 21-22).

Second, it must be stressed that God is still one. In confessing belief in the Trinity Christians do not believe in three gods. This would be tritheism. As the **Baptist Faith and Message** states it, the Father, Son, and Holy Spirit is "without division of nature, essence, or being." This simply affirms that there is but one God.

This threeness-in-one concept of God is without doubt the one concept of God which distinguished Christianity from all other religions. One Christian writer has called it "the ultimate and supreme glory of the Christian faith." And that it is!

## 12. CREATOR OF HEAVEN AND EARTH

Among the most basic affirmations of the Christian faith is that God is Creator of heaven and earth. It is no accident that the Bible opens with the words: "In the beginning God created the heavens and the earth" (Gen. 1:1). The truth expressed in these words is stated and assumed throughout the rest of Scripture. It is the gateway to all divine truth.

### The Author of Creation
The author of creation is clearly God, and He only. "In the beginning GOD created. . ." We are assured, also, that all the "persons" of the Godhead were involved in this creating. Thát the Father is Creator there can be no doubt (Mt. 11: 25; Acts 4: 24; Heb. 1: 2). However, it is equally clear that it was through the agency of the Son that He made all things (Jn. 1:2; Eph. 3:9; Col. 1: 15-16; Heb. 1:2). And it was the Spirit who moved upon the "face of the deep" and brought order of the formless matter (Gen. 1:2; cf. Jb. 26: 13; 33: 4).

### The Scope of Creation
God created "the heavens and the earth". This is a comprehensive expression which means everything. The New Testament enforces this statement by stating that God "created heaven, and the things that therein are, and the earth, and the things that therein are, and the sea, and the things that therein are"

(Rev. 10:6; cf. Acts 4:24). In other words, everything that is. The teaching of the Bible, then, is quite explicit. God, who Himself has no beginning (Psa. 90:2), is the beginning of everything that is.

### The Method of Creation
It is often said that while the Bible affirms the fact of creation it does not tell how God did it. This is not quite true. We are told, for example, that God created what is by His spoken word (cf. Gen. 1:3,6). The method was thus that of divine **fiat**; that is, it was done at once by the mighty power of God, by His all-commanding will and word (Psa. 33:9; Heb. 11:3).

### The Time of Creation
Creation is not dated in the Bible. The Genesis account simply states, "In the beginning God created. . ." The only thing that we can affirm is that there was a beginning. In other words there was a point in God's own life when He decided to call into existence something other than Himself. God Himself has no beginning, but the created order does. This means that God's creation is finite. Matter is not eternal. It had a beginning.

### The Purpose of Creation
The ultimate end of all created things is to glorify God, the Creator, and His Son, Jesus Christ. "The Lord hath made all things for Himself" (Prov. 16: 4). The created order reveals His glory and handiwork (Psa. 19: 1), His wisdom (Prov. 3: 19-20), and His "eternal power and Godhead" (Rom. 1:20). A subordinate or secondary end of creation is for the benefit and good of man. While man himself is a part of God's creation, the rest of creation is for him (Gen. 1: 14-18, 28-31).

### The Implications of Creation
The doctrine of creation has important implications for our views of God, man, and nature. It means that God is independent of the world, but the world is dependent on God. The world is sustained and controlled by God. The world belongs to God. We are but stewards of God's world and must give account to Him for the way in which we use or abuse His creation. The creation is never to take the place of the Creator (Rom. 1: 25).

# Part III


## THE DOCTRINE OF CHRIST

## 13. INTRODUCTION

No doctrine is more important to the Christian faith than the doctrine about Christ. Liberal theologians have thought it possible to separate Christ from Christianity. The essence of Christianity, they say, is simply Christ's message about God and the infinite value of the human soul. One can accept these ideas and ideals of Jesus without coming to any definite conclusion as to the person of Jesus himself.

In other words, it is not necessary to believe anything about Jesus in order to be a Christian; it is only necessary that we share the faith of Jesus. Many who follow this line of thought would not hesitate to say that their moral and religious life would not suffer, even if it should be discovered that Christ never lived. Liberal theology would say that it is possible to have a Christless Christianity.

It should be obvious to all who are acquainted with the New Testament that the above construction is not Christianity at all. A Christless Christianity is a contradiction of terms. You may indeed have religion without Christ; but it is a religion other than New Testament Christianity. According to the New Testament, Christ is the very heart and core of Christianity. Christianity is Christ; Christ is Christianity. Apart from the love and worship of Christ Christianity ceases to exist. The two are absolutely inseparable.

This inseparable relationship between Christ and Christianity makes it differ from all other religions. A noted Christian scholar has observed that "Christianity is the only religion in the world which rests on the Person of its Founder." Take Buddha out of Buddhism or Mohammed out of Islam and nothing essential is lost. You do not, for instance, have to believe anything about Buddha or Mohammed in order to be a Buddhist or Muslim. All that is necessary is to ascribe to their teachings.

It is different, however, with Christ and Christianity. Unlike the founders of the above religions and others, Christ is more than the founder of Christianity who left us his teachings and pointed out a way to God. He claimed to be that Way! Take Christ out of Christianity and everything is lost. If there is, therefore, one doctrine of the Christian faith which is basic to all the others it is the doctrine of Christ.

Generally speaking, most discussions of the doctrine of Christ usually center around two basic questions: (1) Who is Christ? and (2) What is the nature of his work? The first has to do with the **Person of Christ** and the second has to do with the **Work of Christ**.

Christians insist that it makes all the difference in the world as to how one answers these questions. It makes a difference to

Christians; for if Christ is not who he said he was and he did not do what he said he came to do, then the very foundations of the Christian faith are destroyed. It makes a difference to non-Christians; for the way a person answers these questions will determine whether or not he becomes a Christian and will consequently determine his final destiny.

## 14. THE HUMANITY OF CHRIST

It was stated in the last study that the doctrine of Christ is usually divided into two areas of study--the Person of Christ and the Work of Christ. The Person of Christ deals with the question, Who is Jesus? This study deals with a part of the answer to that question.

Who is Jesus? To answer this question fully would require a lengthy volume. Most everything that needs to be said in answer to this question, however, may be discussed under two statements: (1) Jesus was a man, and (2) Jesus was God.

Jesus was a man. This is the logical beginning place in a study of Christ. It is the natural order. Jesus' immediate disciples first knew him as a man, then later as more than a man (Jn. 1: 45-51; 4: 29). This is how we are introduced to him in the New Testament. In considering Jesus as a man two features need emphasis:

### A Real Man

First, Christ's humanity was real. The **Baptist Faith and Message** seeks to emphasize this truth when it states that Christ took "upon Himself the demands and necessities of human nature and identifying Himself completely with mankind" (Art. II, B). This truth is so evident in the New Testament that it hardly needs proving. Yet, since this truth in past centuries has been denied, and Christ's humanity is of such importance, some statements of proof seem justified.

The evidence for Jesus' humanity in the New Testament is abundant. He experienced mental, physical, religious, and social growth as a man (Lk. 2:52). The New Testament describes him as showing the physical reactions of a man, such as, fatigue (Jn. 4:6), sleep (Mt. 8:24), hunger (Mt. 21:18), thirst (Jn. 19:28), and suffering (Mt. 27:19).

Christ also experienced the emotional reactions of a man. He was moved with compassion (Lk. 7:13) and wept (Lk. 19: 41). He grieved and expressed indignation and anger (Mk. 3:5). He knew both joy and sorrow (Jn. 15: 11; Mt. 26: 37). These and other human traits ascribed to him demonstrate that the New Testament everywhere assumes that Jesus was a real man.

## A Unique Man

The second thing to be said about Jesus' humanity concerns its uniqueness. Though real, Christ's humanity is set apart from all other men. As a man he differed from all others in at least two respects.

First, Christ's humanity had a unique origin. According to both of the only two accounts of Christ's birth, there was something supernatural surrounding it. His conception was not according to the ordinary laws of heredity. He had no human father. He was conceived by the Holy Spirit into the womb of the virgin Mary who had never known a man sexually. He was virgin born (see Mt. 1: 18-25; Lk. 1: 26-38).

Second, Christ's humanity differed from all other men in that he was sinless. Jesus himself claimed to be sinless. He challenged others to convince him of sin (Jn. 8: 46). He taught others to confess their sins and pray for forgiveness (Mt. 6:12; Lk. 11: 4), but he himself never confessed sin or asked for forgiveness.

Others recognized his sinlessness. Paul states that he became sin for us but he himself knew no sin (2 Cor. 5:21). The Book of Hebrews states that he was tempted, yet without sin (Heb. 4: 15). Peter called him the righteous dying for the unrighteous (I Pe. 3: 18). John also says he is the righteous one whose blood cleans from all sin (I Jn. 1: 7; 2:1) The **Baptist Faith and Message** simply affirms the New Testament witness by stating that Christ identified "Himself completely with mankind yet without sin."

## 15. THE DEITY OF CHRIST

Jesus was a man, but that is not all. Jesus was also God. He was God manifest in the flesh (I Tim. 3: 16). What a thought! "Christ is the eternal Son of God" is how the **Baptist Faith and Message affirms this truth of the deity of Christ.**

..In discussing the deity of Christ it is necessary at the outset to explain what is meant by the term "deity of Christ." The Christian meaning is quite clear. Christians believe, in the first place, that there is a personal God, the Creator, Redeemer, Preserver, and Ruler of the universe, who is infinite in holiness and all other perfections. So when we say that Jesus is God we simply mean that the same historical Jesus of Nazareth existed in eternity, before he became a man, as infinite eternal God, the second person of the Trinity.

## Christ's Deity Denied

In past centuries certain groups within Christianity questioned the humanity of Jesus. Today, no thoughtful person wishes to deny that Jesus was a real man. In our day it is the deity of Christ, as defined above, which is being questioned. Working under rationalistic and anti-supernaturalistic presuppositions, liberal theologians have been denying for a number of years the true godhood of Jesus. To a great extent, with the help of such popular expressions as the rock opera **Jesus Christ Superstar**, they have succeeded in convincing a great number of people that Jesus was only a man, and a frustrated one at that.

To accept the liberal view of Jesus which denies his deity is to reject the plain teaching of the Bible. The biblical evidence is abundant and convincing. It is not possible nor necessary to state all the evidence within the limits of this study. We will thus limit our remarks to the following line of evidence.

### Jesus' Own Claims

First, Jesus himself claimed to be divine. He claimed to have a unique relationship to the Father (Lk. 2: 49; Jn. 5: 17; 10:30). To know Jesus was to know God (Jn. 8: 19; 14: 9). He made the astounding claim to pre-existence (Jn. 8: 51-58). He accepted Thomas' designation, "My Lord and my God!", and permitted him to worship him (Jn. 20: 26-29). He claimed several prerogatives which belong only to God: the power to forgive sins (Mk. 2: 1-12), the power to bestow life (Jn. 6: 35), absolute authority and power (Mt. 28: 18), and the object of religious faith (Jn. 14: 1).

### Jesus' Followers

Second, Jesus' followers claimed he was divine. This is the unanimous conclusion of all the biblical writers. Lack of space forbids mentioning all the writers, thus we give only a few as examples. John states he existed in the beginning with God and as God (Jn. 1: 1-2). Paul, John, and the writer of Hebrews all affirm that he had part in the creation (Col. 1: 16; Jn. 1: 2; Heb. 1:2). Paul in addition says he is "the image of the invisible God" (Col. 1: 15), "the fullness of the Godhead bodily" (Col. 2:9), and "God manifest in the flesh" (I Tim. 3: 16). Peter equates him with God (II Pe. 1:1).

### Jesus' Deeds

Third, Christ validated his claims to deity by his deeds of divine power. In the mouth of any other person Jesus' claims would appear to be either inexcusable conceit or madness. But in the mouth of Jesus they seem reasonable and fitting. Why? Because he backed them up with his divine power. He demonstrated his power over sickness and disease, over nature, and over life and death itself. Despite the vigorous attempts of liberalism, it has been impossible to eliminate these supernatural elements from Jesus' life.

The one deed which demonstrates finally and conclusively Christ's claim to deity is his resurrection. Death could not hold him. He rose from the dead and showed himself alive by many "infallible proofs" (Acts 1:3). Because of this we may be sure that Jesus was who he said he was, the "I AM" who existed before Abraham was. Amen!

## 16. THE REDEMPTIVE WORK OF CHRIST

It was noted in a previous study that the doctrine of Christ is usually divided into two parts: (1) the Person of Christ and (2) the Work of Christ. The last studies were devoted to the person of Christ. We now turn to the work of Christ.

The work of Christ is concerned with what Jesus came to the earth to do. Of course, he did many things. He went about teaching, preaching, and healing (Mt. 4: 23). To tell everything Jesus did would, as John says, fill the world with books (Jn. 21: 25). We are concerned here with only his primary mission and accomplishment.

What was Christ's primary work? Some have mistakenly thought that his primary accomplishment was that he left us a body of moral and religious instruction. Others have erroneously thought that his primary work was that of a social and political reformer. It is particularly fasionable today to put Jesus in this mould.

Christ was not primarily a teacher nor a reformer. If these were his primary aims, then the humbling of himself to become a man need not have taken place at all. The law of Moses left us adequate moral instruction, and the prophets had already spoken out eloquently against social evils. If ethical instruction and social reformation were Christ's major accomplishments then his coming was unnecessary and his work a failure.

What then was Christ's primary work? The New Testament answer is clear. His primary work was redemptive. Christ came into the world primarily to give God's solution to the sin problem. This mission included two great objectives: (1) the removal of the penalty which came upon man as a result of sin, and (2) the restoration of men to the image and fellowship of God. Both of these objectives were essential to his redemptive work.

Everything Christ did was related to his work of redemption. We may, however, summarize this work with three events: his death, his resurrection, and his ascension.

## Christ's Death

The death of Christ is, without doubt, his central redemptive event. It is not putting the matter too strongly to say that the very purpose for which Christ came into the world was to die (Mk. 10: 45; Heb. 2:14). It is through Christ's death that our salvation is made possible, for in his death Christ paid the penalty for man's sin (II Cor. 5:21; Heb. 2:9). As the **Baptist Faith and Message** states it: "In His death on the cross He made provision for redemption of men from sin."

## Christ's Resurrection

Christ's resurrection was also an essential part of his redemptive work. It is through his resurrection that we have assurance of salvation. By raising Christ from the dead God demonstrated that his redemptive work was accepted (Rom. 1: 4; 4: 25; Acts 10: 4-43). It also gives us assurance that God will complete our salvation by raising us from the dead, and that the kingdom of God will triumph (I Cor. 15: 12-28).

## Christ's Ascension

Christ's redemptive work did not end with his death and resurrection. He ascended to the right hand of God where he now makes intercession for us (Rom. 8: 34; Heb. 7: 25). This is Christ's present and continuous work for us. It is this work which gives us confidence in prayer (Heb. 4: 14-16), and guarantees our permanent standing before God. (I Jn. 2 : 1).

Christ died for our sins, he was raised for our justification, he now lives to make intercession for us. This is his redemptive work.

## 17. IS JESUS THE ONLY WAY TO GOD?

Is Jesus the only way to God? To put it another way, Is there only one way to be saved? This question is being asked more and more by this generation. There are three movements in contemporary religious life which make it exceedingly important that we know the answer.

### Important Issue

First, there is the syncretistic tendency in religious life today. Syncretism is an attempt to unite all religions--Christian and non-Christian--into one universal religion. This is the stated goal of some leaders within the ecumenical movement. The idea is that one religion is as good as the other. All of them contain both good and bad elements. What is needed is to pick out the good in each one and form one good religion.

Another movement is called universalism. This is the belief that all people will eventually be saved. Naturally, according to this view, Jesus is not the only way to God. God is the Father of all of us. One hears this view expressed in the often stated doctrine of the "Fatherhood of God and the brotherhood of man."

A third factor in the religious scene is the missionary activity of the non-Christian religions. For the first time, at least in this part of the world, the non-Christian religions are actively seeking converts. Representatives of other religions are especially active on college campuses. This is causing many young people to be confronted anew with the question, Is Jesus really the only way to God? Perhaps he is only one of many ways?

## Jesus' Claims

There can be no doubt about the claims of Jesus himself. Perhaps the clearest statement is found in John 14: 6: "I am the way, and the truth, and the life; no one comes to the Father, but by me." This statement, especially the latter part, constitutes an unequivocal exclusive claim that there is no other way to God. Added to this is the statement that "neither knoweth any man the Father, save the Son and he to whomsoever the Son will reveal him" (Mt. 11: 27), and also the stern warning in I Jn. 2:23: "Whosoever denieth the Son, the same hath not the Father."

The consistent teaching of these and other statements is quite clear. There is no other way that a person can come to a personal knowledge of, and fellowship with, God, but through Jesus Christ.

## Apostles' Claims

The preaching of the apostles is as clear as the claims of Jesus on this issue. Peter, speaking to the Jews, said: "Neither is there salvation in any other: for there is none other name under heaven given among men, whereby we must be saved" (Acts 4: 12). Paul, speaking to the Gentiles, said: "through this man is preached unto you the forgiveness of sins: And by him all that believe are justified" (Acts 13: 38, 39).

It should be kept in mind that both the Jews and Gentiles were religious. The Gentiles had their gods, and the Jews believed in the God of the Old Testament. Yet this was not sufficient. There is salvation only in Jesus.

To say that Jesus is the only way to God seems to be so intolerant to this broadminded age. Yet it is the historic Christian position. It is the teaching of Jesus and the apostles. To deny it is to be less than Christian. Indeed, any other answer is not a Christian answer.

Part IV


# THE DOCTRINE OF THE HOLY SPIRIT

# 18. INTRODUCTION

God has revealed himself as Father, Son, and Holy Spirit. That is, God is triune in his nature. In these doctrinal studies we have now come to consider the "Third Person" of the Godhead--the Holy Spirit.

In the history of Christian Doctrine there has always been two extremes when it comes to the doctrine of the Holy Spirit. From ancient to modern times some have so emphasized the Spirit to the extent that the person of Christ and his redemptive work were pushed into a secondary place of importance. The groups who have fallen into this error are also quite frequently characterized by emotional excesses in the expression of their Christian experience. The other extreme is that others have placed little or no emphasis on the Holy Spirit.

Of the two extremes it is probably true that the Holy Spirit has been more often neglected than over-emphasized. Like the Ephesians a great number of people within professing Christianity have not so much as even heard whether there be a Holy Spirit (Acts 19: 1-2). So prevalent has been this neglect in a wide segment of Christianity that the Holy Spirit has been called "the neglected person in the Godhead."

At the present time, however, the doctrine of the Spirit is receiving great attention among Christian thinkers and workers. It may even be said that no longer is the Holy Spirit "the neglected person in the Godhead." There seems to be more preaching on the subject from the pulpit than there has been in a long time. Spiritual life conferences in which the person and work of the Spirit are emphasized are common occurrences today. Hosts of people who have been Christians for a long time are for the first time being introduced to the "Spirit-filled life."

This renewed interest in the doctrine of the Holy Spirit should be welcomed by all who are concerned about the powerlessness and worldliness in the church today. The current interest in the Holy Spirit is not without its dangers, of course. We may very easily fall into the error of over-emphasis or, worst still, a wrong emphasis. There must be, therefore, a strict adherence to what the Scriptures actually teach about the Spirit and his relationship to the church and to the individual believer.

In the past Baptists have had a strong and balanced view of the Holy Spirit. In the **Baptist Faith and Message** a brief but very comprehensive paragraph is devoted to the doctrine of the Holy Spirit. In it the work of the Holy Spirit in conversion, in the development of Christian character, and in the bestowal of power for service, is stressed.

It is no doubt  true that the excesses which are sometimes associated with an emphasis on the Holy Spirit have caused many Baptists to neglect the scriptural teaching on the subject. Like some other groups, though, many Baptist people are beginning to have a renewed interest in learning  about the Spirit. Because of this interest, and also because some have already fallen prey to some of the dangers often connected with the subject, we will devote the next several studies to the Holy Spirit.

## 19. THE PERSON OF THE HOLY SPIRIT

Like the doctrine of Christ, it is common to divide the doctrine of the Holy Spirit into two areas: (1) the Person of the Holy Spirit and (2) the Work of the Holy Spirit. In other words, we are concerned with who the Holy Spirit is, and with what he does. This study is concerned with the question, Who is the Holy Spirit? In answering this question two points need emphasizing.

### The Personality of the Holy Spirit

First, the Holy Spirit is a person. When we deal with the Spirit of God we must realize that he is not some impersonal force or influence; neither is he some sort of nebulous, vague substance. The Spirit is revealed to us in the Scriptures and in our own Christian experience as personal.

It is strange that the personality of the Holy Spirit should need special emphasis in our discussion of him. But it does. Despite the clear teaching of the Bible, especially the  New Testament, a surprisingly large number of Christians still refer to the Spirit as an "it." It is necessary to state, therefore, the biblical evidence for speaking of the Holy Spirit specifically and distinctly as a real person. The evidence may be summarized around two statements:

First, the Holy Spirit is spoke of in personal terms. The clearest example of this is in Jesus' farewell address as recorded in John 14-16. Here Jesus calls the Holy Spirit the "Comforter", the one who would take his place in guiding the disciples. As Jesus had comforted and guided them up to this point; so the Holy Spirit is now to take his place.

This is clearly no impersonal influence or power who is to be the companion and guide to the disciples in the place of Jesus. This other comforter is to be a real person like Jesus himself. To reinforce this truth Jesus consistently uses the masculine personal pronoun to refer to him (he always uses "he" or "him", never "it"; cf. Jn. 16: 8, 13, 14).

Second, the Spirit is spoken of as having personal qualities. Throughout the entire Bible the Spirit of God is always thought of as having personal attributes, performing personal functions, and entering into personal relationships. He has all the necessary attributes of a person: knowledge (I Cor. 2:10), will (I Cor. 12:11), affection (II Tim. 1: 7), and moral appreciation (Jn. 16: 9).

The Holy Spirit exercises the functions of a person; such as, hearing (Jn. 16: 13), speaking (Acts 10: 19), teaching (Lk. 12: 12), praying (Ro. 8: 26), forbidding (Acts 16: 6-7), comforting (Acts 9: 31), guiding (Jn. 16: 16), revealing (Jn. 16: 14), and calling into the work of the Lord (Acts 13: 2). He also experienced as a person. In his relationship to persons he can be grieved (Eph. 4: 30), resisted (Acts 7: 51), sinned against (Mt. 12: 31), lied to (Acts 5:3), rebelled against (Is. 63: 10), and insulted (Heb. 10: 29).

### The Deity of the Holy Spirit
The second point needing emphasis is that the Holy Spirit is not only a person, he is God. The title "Holy Spirit" is especially appropriate in emphasizing his deity. In a former study we noted that the word "holy" in the Old Testament is practically synonymous with deity. Furthermore, the Holy Spirit is distinctly called God (Acts 5:4), and the attributes of God are ascribed to him. He is eternal (He. 9: 14), omipresent (Psa. 139: 7-10), omnipotent (Lk. 1: 35), and omniscient (I Cor. 2: 10-11).

Who is the Holy Spirit? He is a real person; he is God. He is the Third Person of the Triune Godhead.


## 20. THE WORK OF THE HOLY SPIRIT

The Holy Spirit has always been at work. Beginning with the creation he was at work throughout the Old Testament period (Gen.. 1:2; 6:3; Ex. 28:3; I Sam. 10:6; Ez. 2:2). It is in the New Testament, however, that the distinctive work of the Holy Spirit is made clear. In a general way we may say that the New Testament emphasizes a three-fold relationship in the mission and function of the Spirit's work today.

### In The World
First, there is the work of the Spirit in relationship to the world. By "world" we mean humankind, and in particular, unregenerate humanity in distinction from believers (cf. Jn. 3:16; 16:8). Jesus said: "When he is come, he will reprove the world . . ." (Jn. 16:8).

The word "reprove" means here to convict, or to convince. Thus it is the work of the Holy Spirit to make men realize their lost condition and make them seek after life and righteousness.

But the Spirit does not simply convict men and leave it at that. He gives life. He quickens men and creates the disposition and power in the sinner's heart to believe in Christ for salvation. Thus the work of the Holy Spirit in relationship to the world is two-fold: he convicts of sin and he regenerates.

### In Believers

Second, there is the work of the Holy Spirit in relationship to believers. The Holy Spirit works in the life of the individual believer and in the life of the church. In the case of the individual believer there is a work which the Spirit does at conversion and is never repeated; then there is a work of the Spirit which he does after conversion which is continuous.

At conversion the Holy Spirit indwells the believer (I Cor. 6:19); he seals the believer unto the day of final redemption (II Cor. 1:22; Eph. 1:13; 4:30), and he baptizes the believer into the body of Christ (I Cor. 12:13). All of these acts are once and for all and are not repeated.

After conversion the Spirit continues to work in and for the believer. He cultivates Christian character, brings comfort (Jn. 14:15-17), teaches and helps the believer understand the word of God (Jn. 16:13; I Cor. 2:13-15). Furthermore, he empowers the believer for service (Lk. 24:49) Acts 1:8). This is especially important to remember, for only as one submits to the control of the Holy Spirit can there be any real power for service to God and man.

But the Spirit not only works in and for the individual believer, he works in the life of the fellowship of believers - the church. It is the Spirit who creates the unity of the body (Eph. 4:3). It is through the Spirit that true worship is possible (Jn. 4:24; Phil 3:3; Eph. 6:18). He is the one who gives the necessary gifts for the ministry and for the edification of the church (Eph. 4:8-12; I Cor. 12:4-11).

### Relationship to Christ

Finally, there is the work of the Holy Spirit in relationship to Christ. There was a close relationship of the Spirit to the earthly life of Jesus. However, we are interested here in his relationship to Christ today. In short, the Spirit does two things in reference to Jesus. He glorifies Christ (Jn. 16:14), and he makes Christ real to the believer. It is important to keep these facts in mind. Any experience or emphasis on the Holy Spirit which is genuine and biblical will never push Christ into the background.

## 21. THE WORK OF THE HOLY SPIRIT
## IN CONVERSION

There is no other work of the Holy Spirit which needs more emphasis today than his work in conversion. Much of the current emphasis on the Holy Spirit is devoted to his work in the believer after conversion. The Bible has a great deal to say about this, and it is thus a legitimate emphasis. However, hardly anything is being said about the work of the Spirit in becoming a Christian.

The **Baptist Faith and Message** states that the Holy Spirit "convicts of sin, of righteousness and of judgment. He calls men to the Saviour, and effects regeneration" (Art. II, C). This statement affirms a two-fold work of the Spirit in connection with becoming a Christian. He convicts, and he regenerates.

### Conviction

First, the Holy Spirit convicts the sinner. He awakens the sinner to his need of salvation (Jn. 16:8-11). The Bible teaches us that the sinner is "dead in trespasses and sin" (Eph. 2:1). This means that, left to himself, the sinner would not desire to make even the motion of turning from sin, nor would he be able (Jn. 6:44).

It is very easy to go astray at this point. We may be led to believe at times that powerful preaching and persuasive pleading are the means by which men are convicted. These may be means the Spirit uses, but it must ever be kept in mind that it is the Spirit who convicts men. If the Spirit does not convict, there is nothing that man can do to bring about that result.

Every preacher of the gospel knows the frustrating experience of proclaiming the good news of salvation to people who do not want to be saved. Even our preaching must be done in the power of the Spirit (I Cor. 2:4; I Thes. 1:5). It is thus very important and necessary that we understand that God's Spirit must convict if men are to be stirred enough to want to be saved.

### Regeneration

But the Spirit not only convicts, he also regenerates. Regeneration is simply the imparting of spiritual life in the heart of the sinner. Through this work of the Spirit man is given the desire and the power to turn from his sins and receive Christ as Saviour.

This regenerating work of God's Spirit is an absolute necessity if man is to be saved (Jn. 3:3, 5). By himself man can never turn to God. We have noted that he is dead in trespasses and sins (Eph. 2:1). It is useless to bid a physically dead man to get up and live. Shout as we will, he cannot hear. A similar situation exists in the realm of the spirit.

Hence, unregenerate man is utterly unable to turn to God and do good. He cannot think his way to God for sin has darkened his understanding (Eph. 4:18) and his natural mind cannot receive or know the things of God (I Cor. 2:14). He cannot will his way to God for he is a bondservant of sin (Jn. 8:34) and a child of disobedience (Eph. 2:2). He cannot use his emotions to love God because the natural man is at "enmity against God" (Rom. 8:7).

In short, spiritual life is the work of the Spirit and not a natural achievement. Man's pride sometimes deceives him into thinking that it is through his own strong arm that he has come to God. But spiritually dead people cannot quicken themselves. This is the sovereign work of God's Spirit (Eph. 2:1, 5; Col. 2:13).

## 22. THE WORK OF THE SPIRIT IN THE CHRISTIAN

The work of the Holy Spirit in the life of an individual does not end with conversion. He does a great deal more in and for the believer after conversion. Many terms and expressions are used in the New Testament to describe this relationship of the Spirit to the believer. As helpful and instructive as it would be, we cannot discuss or even mention all of these terms here. We do plan to discuss some of them in detail in future studies, but for our purposes here we will summarize the work of the Spirit in the life of the believer in the following manner.

### Indwelling
First, the Spirit indwells the believer. At conversion the Spirit takes up residence in the believer. Our bodies become the temple of the Holy Spirit (I Cor. 3:16, 6:19), and he "dwelleth in us" (II Tim. 1:14; cf. Jn. 14:17). This means every believer, for "if any man have not the Spirit of Christ, he is none of his" (Rom. 8:9). Thus, all believers, no matter how weak and imperfect they may be, have the Spirit dwelling in them.

This indwelling of the Spirit is a permanent thing. He comes to abide with the believer forever (Jn. 14:16). This is a precious truth. It means that the Christian is never separated from the indwelling presence of God. God is always with us to supply our every need. It means that we can enjoy the constant companionship and fellowship of God.

### Empowering
Second, the Holy Spirit empowers the believer for service. This note of power runs all the way through the New Testament. Jesus himself knew this power, for "God anointed him with the Holy Ghost

and with power" (Acts 10:38). The disciples were to wait until they were "endued with power" (Lk. 24:49). The power to carry out Christ's commission of evangelizing the world was to come from the Holy Spirit (Acts 1:8). The ministry and preaching of the apostles was performed in the power of the Spirit (Acts 3:12; Rom. 15:19; I Cor. 2:4f).

The power of the Spirit was thus a characteristic feature of early Christianity. However, this power was not for them only, but to all them who believe (Acts 2:39; II Tim. 1:7). This includes believers today.

### Christian Character

Third, the Holy Spirit enables the believer to live the Christian life. As the **Baptist Faith and Message** puts it, the Spirit "cultivates Christian character." That is, the Spirit produces in the believer those Christian graces which make the Christian Christ-like; such as, "love, joy, peace, longsuffering, gentleness, goodness, faith, meekness, temperance" (Gal. 5:22; cf. Rom. 15:13). These graces are the fruit of the Spirit and cannot come just through human effort.

This enabling power of the Spirit is a distinguishing mark of the Christian faith. Other religions tell what a person should do and be. However, the Christian message is not one which simply tells us what we ought to do and be; it tells us of a power by which we can do it. It is through God's Spirit.

### Guidance

Fourth, the Holy Spirit guides the believer. Everyone knows the experience of having to make a decision when he is confused as to what line to take. This can be one of the most perplexing moments in life. The Christian has the wonderful promise that the Holy Spirit will guide him "into all truth" (Jn. 16:13). The Spirit gives us words necessary when we need help (Mk. 13:11), he will guide us to solutions of difficult problems (Acts 15:28), and he will show us the way we should go (Acts 16:6ff.).

The closer we are to God, the more we know the reality of the Spirit's guidance. Too frequently, I fear, our spiritual lives are too dim to discern the Spirit's guidance. But his guidance is available. Let us stay close to him so that he may be able to lead us in his will and way.

## 23. THE WORK OF THE HOLY SPIRIT IN THE CHURCH

The work of the Holy Spirit in the corporate life of the church is often overlooked. His work is often thought of only in relationship to individual believers. Of course, the church is made up of individual believers, and in one sense there can be no arbitrary distinction between the work of the Spirit in the believer and the work of the Spirit in the church. Nevertheless, there is a definite work of the Spirit in reference to believers as a group, that is the corporate life of the church.

## Fellowship

In the first place, it is the Holy Spirit who creates the fellowship of the church. In two places in the New Testament the "fellowship of the Spirit" is mentioned (II Cor. 13:14; Phil. 2:1). While this expression may mean "participation in the Holy Spirit," it may also mean "fellowship created by the Holy Spirit." Possibly both ideas are represented in the phrase. Whatever its exact meaning, it is beyond doubt that the New Testament views the church as a fellowship of redeemed people called into being by the Holy Spirit.

## Worship

Second, the Holy Spirit inspires and guides the worship of the church. Worship is often considered to be merely an activity of the human spirit. It is that. Unfortunately, it all too frequently amounts to that only. The New Testament teaches us that true worship is primarily a spiritual activity (Jn. 4:24). Paul explicitly states that a distinguishing mark of God's people is that they "worship by the Spirit of God" (Phil. 3:3). Specific acts of worship are attributed to the Holy Spirit. The Spirit inspires singing and praise (I Cor. 14:26; Eph. 5:18-20). Preaching and teaching are to be done in the power of the Spirit (I Cor. 2:4; Acts 4:31). Prayer is especially singled out as an activity of the Spirit (Rom. 8:26-27; Eph. 6:18).

This is an important truth to keep in mind when we try to "plan" our worship services. As W. T. Conner reminds us, "The church that makes out its program of worship without reference to the Holy Spirit forgets what worship is and what it is for." All too often form, ritual, and entertainment (in these days, especially entertainment), take the place of the spiritual in worship. None of these make worship, and are often even hindrances to true worship. To be acceptable to God, worship must rely upon the inspiration and power of the Spirit of God.

## Equiping Church

Third, the Spirit equips the church for its mission and ministry. He does this by giving the necessary "gifts" to the church. There are some twenty gifts listed in three key passages in the New Testament (Rom. 12:6-8; I Cor. 12:4-11, 28-30; Eph. 4:7-12). The meaning of some of these is obscure, and there has been much dispute as to their place and importance in the church today.

Here we need only emphasize that these gifts are bestowed by the Holy Spirit (I Cor. 12:11). They are not natural abilities. They are not given because of human merit or seeking. They are not given for the purpose of personal enjoyment. The gifts are given freely by the Spirit to whomsoever he wills, and they are meant to be used in the service of the whole church (I Cor. 12:7).

In summary, the church could not exist without the Holy Spirit. He calls it into being; he creates its fellowship and worship; he equips it for its ministry. Without the Spirit the church would never have been, and without him it would cease to exist tomorrow.

## 24. THE BAPTISM AND FULLNESS OF THE SPIRIT

**The Baptist Faith and Message** contains no reference to the baptism of the Spirit nor to the fullness of the Spirit. However, probably more Baptists today are concerned and confused about the meaning of these two terms than any other aspect of the doctrine of the Holy Spirit. Much is being said and written on both of these topics today. In light of this we close out our studies on the Holy Spirit with this brief discussion of this particular activity of the Spirit.

### Baptism of the Spirit

There are seven references to the baptism with the Spirit in the New Testament. Four of these record the prophecy of John the Baptist that Jesus would baptize with the Spirit (Mt. 3:11; Mk. 1:8; Lk. 3:16; Jn. 1:33). The fifth is Jesus' quotation of this same prophecy which he applies to Pentecost (Acts 1:5). The sixth is Peter's quotation of Jesus which he applies to the conversion of Cornelius and to Pentecost (Acts 11:16-17). The seventh is in I Cor. 12:13, in which Paul states that all believers have been baptized with the same Spirit.

Much could and probably should be said about each of these references. However, the limits of this study permit us to make only the following observations: (1) In none of these references is there any indication that one is to "seek" the baptism with the Spirit. (2) None of these references give any indication that the believer should look for a "sign," such as speaking in tongues, as an evidence that he has received the baptism. (3) The baptism of the Spirit is something all believers have received and share in common.

I am aware that the baptism with the Spirit is a matter concerning which many sincere Christians disagree. Nevertheless, the

Scriptural evidence leads this writer to the following conclusion. The Baptism with the Spirit is an experience which happens to all believers at conversion. It is the one act of the Spirit which puts the believer into the Spiritual body of Christ.

### Filling of the Spirit

In the case of the fullness of the Spirit it is a different matter. The believer is commanded to be "filled with the Spirit" (Eph. 5:18). This command implies at least three things about the fullness of the Spirit.

First, it indicates that some Christians are not filled with the Spirit. If all believers are already filled with the Spirit, then the command is pointless. Second, it tells us that all believers are expected to be filled with the Spirit. The fullness of the Spirit is not some special experience for a select group. Third, the fullness of the Spirit is something which needs repeated and maintained. This thought is supported by the verb tense in the command and the examples we have in the Acts (cf. Acts 2:4 with Acts 4:31).

### Conclusion

In comparing the two terms, then, we may say that all believers have been baptized with the Spirit, but not all are filled with the Spirit. The baptism with the Spirit is a once-for-all-never-to-be-repeated experience which takes place at conversion. The filling of the Spirit is the continuing relationship of the believer with the Holy Spirit after conversion.

The question to be asked a believer, therefore, is not, "Have you been baptized with the Spirit? The question is, "Are you filled with the Spirit?" It is feared that many Christians are unable to answer this question. They either do not know what it means or they do not know how to tell whether they have been filled or not.

The fullness of the Spirit is simply a matter of being controlled or possessed by the Spirit. The way one may know is to examine his life for the fruits. Marks of the Spirit's fullness are made plain in the Scriptures: boldness in witnessing (Acts 4:31), gladness and joy in worship (Eph. 5:19-20), and a Christ-like character (Gal. 5:22-23). There is no doubt that these marks are missing in many Christians. So, the command "be filled with the Spirit" needs heeded today.

# Part V

## THE DOCTRINE OF MAN AND SIN

# 25. INTRODUCTION

Without a doubt the primary theme of the Bible is God himself. God and his dealings with man is what the Bible is all about. All the previous studies have been devoted to the doctrine of God, all three persons of the triune Godhead--Father, Son, and Holy Spirit. We come now to consider the second most important subject in the Bible--man.

The doctrine of man is an especially relevant subject today. There is currently a lively interest in the subject of human nature. Of course, man has always been concerned about himself. Long ago men were asking, "What is man?" (Psa. 8:4; Jb. 7:17). However, this question seems to be asked by more people today than ever before. Contemporary songs and modern literature deal with some of the most fundamental questions of human existence. What is man? Where did he come from? What is his future? Everyone seems to be asking, "Whom am I?"

Modern scholarship has labored with these questions and have ventured to answer some of them. Philosophers, psychologists, biologists, and theologians have given their opinions as to who and what man is. Anthropologists have tried to tell us where man came from. Much speculation has been made as to the future of man, but no one seems to know for sure.

In all the current interest and discussion about man there is one clear fact which shines through the maze of confusing and conflicting opinions. No one seems to know for sure the answers to the most important questions concerning human existence. There is no sure word about man from modern scholarship. Some of their findings have proved helpful to our total understanding of human nature and behavior. However, to a large extent modern scholarship has come up with no satisfactory answers to the basic questions about man.

The Christian faith has the answers. This is not a presumptuous statement; it is simply an affirmation as to what the Christian religion claims to teach. The God of the Christian Scriptures has not only told us about himself, he has also told us about ourselves. He has told us about where we came from ,what we are, and something about our destiny. The Christian does not have to engage in fanciful speculation nor depend on educated guesses in seeking the answers to these basic questions about man's existence. We have the sourcebook of God's sure Word.

At no period in the history of mankind has there been a greater need to set forth the Christian view of man than in our day. Some modern views of man have made him to be nothing more than an animal. This distortion of the biblical view of human nature has contributed much to many of the problems faced by society today.

## 26. THE ORIGIN OF MAN

Of all the questions relating to man none has interested man more intently than his origin. Theories abound as to how man came to be. Textbooks in the various sciences offer suggestions and make all kinds of speculations as to where man came from.

### Evolutionary View

The most common explanation of the origin of man found in academic circles today is some form of evolution. Among the evolutionists there are two main classes. First, there are the naturalists. These hold that man got here by mere chance. By accident the simplest forms of living matter began through some form of spontaneous generation from dead matter, and from these simple forms of life other more complicated forms of life evolved, and from these man finally evolved.

There is, however, a class of evolutionists known as theists. These accept the evolutionary theory as to the origin of man's body, but deny that it was by chance. Behind the whole process is God. A theistic evolutionist looks upon evolution simply as God's way of bringing man into being.

What is the Christian to say about the evolutionary explanation of man's origin? It cannot be proven, neither is it needed. To give such an answer, to be sure, subjects one to the charge of ignorance. Evolution is the sacred cow of the twentieth century, and anyone who would dare dispute it is considered foolish. It is, nevertheless, only a theory, and Christians need not jump on the bandwagon simply because it is the "intellectual" thing to do. All honest scientists will admit that any theory of evolution is fraught with difficulties and in the end leaves man's origin shrouded in mystery.

### Biblical View

The biblical, and thus Christian, view of man's origin is a great deal more clear and definite, and makes a lot more sense. The biblical passages which deal specifically with the subject are Gen. 1:27; 2:7; Rom. 5:12f; I Cor. 15:24f. Taking the plain, literal meaning of these passages (which is the best and safest method of interpreting the Bible), we arrive at the following account of man's origin. God made man's body from the elements found in the earth, and imparted to him directly spiritual life. From man he made woman, the first pair, and from these two all the human race has descended. This is the plain, unadorned Scripture account. In it three things stand out clearly.

First, man was **created** by God. He is not, therefore, the accidental product of blind chance. He has his origin in the creative activity of God. He is thus a creature, and is not himself independent and free. He is accountable to his Maker.

Second, man was created by a **special** act of God. As the **Baptist Faith and Message** puts it: "Man was created by the special act of God, in His own image, and is the crowning work of creation" (Art. III). This solves the mystery of human existence. This special act of God separates man from beast. He is created in a class by himself. In man is the breath of the Almighty (Gen. 2:7), the image of his Creator (Gen. 1:27). Between the lowest man and the highest developed beast is therefore a gulf which cannot be bridged.

Third, the whole human race sprang from one original pair, or rather one original man. This fact is plainly taught in Genesis and other passages (cf. Acts 17:26), and is assumed throughout the entire biblical record. God's one plan of salvation is predicated on the unity of the human race.


## 27. THE NATURE OF MAN

In the last study we dealt with the fact that God created man. We now turn our attention to how God created him. Just what kind of being is man? What is his make-up? Is man composed of body alone, or is there an aspect of man which is other than body? Is man simply the highest developed animal, or is there something about man which clearly distinguishes him from the beast?

### Composite Creature

The Christian Scriptures clearly teach that man is more than a body. Man is a composite creature; that is, there are two distinct principles or substances in man— his body and his soul. This is made plain in the account of man's creation in Gen. 2:7: "And the Lord God formed man of the dust of the ground, and breathed into his nostrils the breath of life; and man became a living soul." This truth is explicitly taught in many other places in the Bible, and it implicitly underlies all the teaching of the Word of God (cf. Eccl. 12:7; Zech. 12:1; Mt. 10:28; Jn. 12:27; I Cor. 5:3-4; I Thess. 5:23; Heb. 4:12; 12:23; Ja. 2:26).

It is obvious that man has a body. It is only necessary here to stress that the Christian faith holds that the body is a real and essential part of man's nature. It is divinely made, and thus is good and is never to be despised nor downgraded (I Cor. 6:19-20).

But man is more than a body. He is a soul. Admittedly, the soul is difficult to define. It is abundantly clear in the Bible, however, that it is a real substance distinct from the body (Gen. 2:7; Mt. 10:28; Ja. 2:26). It is the life principle of the body, and without it the body would be only clay, lifeless, dead (Ja. 2:7; Ja. 2:26; Eccl. 12:7). Thus, the soul inhabits the body, removes from it at death, and exists in a separate state after death (Phil. 1:20-24; II Cor. 5:8; Rev. 6: 9-10).

### Image of God

In affirming the existence of the soul, it thus follows that man is more than the highest developed animal. Man's body certainly has many things in common with animals. However, man was endowed by his Creator with an element which puts an unbridgeable gulf between him and the highest developed animal. He is said to be created in the "image of God" (Gen. 1:26-27).

The "image of God" in man is as difficult to define as the soul. Some feel that it refers to man's freedom of will; others identify it with man's intelligence; and others his ability to make moral decisions. Perhaps it includes all of these. The one thing that is clear is that the image of God distinguishes man from the rest of God's creatures. None of the others is created in this image. It makes man's life more sacred than the animals and gives him his superiority over the beasts (cf. Gen. 9:1-7).

In short, the image of God consists in the possession of a spiritual nature. Originally, it consisted of a knowledge of God, and gives man, even in his fallen state, a capacity to know and worship God (Col. 3:10). It also consisted of righteousness and holiness, and thus means that man is a moral creature, one who has the capacity for moral choices and actions (Eph. 4:24). Man is not, therefore, simply the highest form of animals; he is a moral and spiritual creature.

In our day, particularly, we need to be reminded that man is more. than a body and an animal. There are powerful tendencies in our culture today which would have us to believe this is all man is. Everything in our world about us is geared to reminding us that we have bodies. Bodies to feed, clothe, and adorn. Many voices tell us on every hand that man is only an animal, and are encouraging us to act the part. As Christians we must ever remind ourselves and others that man is more than body and animal; he is a soul, a moral and spiritual creature responsible to a holy God.

## 28. THE FALL OF MAN

From the first two chapters of the Bible we learn that man was created by God with an upright character, innocent of sin, in fellowship with God, and placed in an environment which was "all very good." However, that original condition soon changed. In Genesis 3 we have the account of how man was tempted to sin by a personal being of another kind, yielded to that temptation, and thus fell from his original state of righteousness.

The event of man's original sin as recorded in Genesis 3 is called the "fall of man." The **Baptist Faith and Message** contains the following statement on this doctrine: "By his free choice man sinned against God and brought sin into the human race. Through the temptation of Satan man transgressed the command of God, and fell from his original innocence; whereby his posterity inherit a nature an an environment inclined toward sin, and as soon as they are capable of moral action become transgressors and are under condemnation" (Art. III). In this summary of man's fall two points need to be especially stressed.

### Historical Event

First, the fall of man was an actual historic act. This means, of course, that Adam was an historical being. It is fashionable in our time to interpret Genesis 1-3 as myth or religious parable. Such a view considers Adam simply as representative man. It denies that he was a person as we are persons and that his history was history as our history is history.

Nevertheless, as difficult as it may be for the modern mind to accept, the first three chapters of Genesis purport to be genuine history. Furthermore, the New Testament recognizes Adam as an historical person (Lk. 3:38; Jude 14; I Cor. 15:45), and acknowledges his transgression as an actual event (Rom 5:12-21). Thus, when we speak of the fall of man we are not simply talking of every man's experience, but the actual act of one individual, whose act in turn brought his descendants into ruin.

### Inherited Depravity

This brings us to the second point to be emphasized in the doctrine of the fall: Adam's sin has affected the whole human race. It has done so in two ways. First, all of Adam's descendants inherit a sinful, corrupt nature. The term "total depravity" is used to describe this result of the fall.

By saying that man is totally depraved we do not mean that every person is as corrupt as he can be. We simply mean that man's whole nature, every element and faculty of his being, has been affected by sin. Consequently, while every person may not be as bad as he possibly can be, he has been so infected with sin that without the restraining power of God he will become worse and worse (Rom. 1:18-32).

It seems to be particularly offensive in these days to speak of man being totally depraved. Those who oppose the terminology usually point out that the Bible never uses the term. This is true, but the idea is certainly there. The Bible everywhere affirms that man's whole nature is corrupt. His mind and understanding is darkened (Eph. 4:18); his heart is corrupt and full of evil (Jer. 17:9; Mt. 15:19); His will is perverted (Rom. 7:15-19); and his affections are alienated from God (Rom. 8:7). Thus there dwells no good thing in man (Rom. 7:18), and no man may be called good (Rom. 3:10; Mk. 10:17).

### Sin Universal

The second effect the fall has had on the whole human race is that sin has become universal. Because of our inherited sinful nature we all commit acts of sin sooner or later. The **Baptist Faith and Message** emphasizes this truth by saying that as soon as we are capable of moral action we "become transgressors and are under condemnation." This means that all human beings, without respect of condition or class, are sinners before God (Rom. 3:19, 23).

That sin is universal is one of the clearest teachings of the Bible. There is no need to discuss it at length. One only needs to read the following biblical passages: I Kgs. 8:46; Ps. 143:2; Eccl. 7:20; Rom. 3:10-19; I Jn. 1:8. But not only does the Bible affirm this truth. Experience, observation, and human history also show there is something fundamentally wrong with mankind.


## 29. THE ORIGIN AND NATURE OF SIN

In the last study we looked at the biblical teaching concerning the fall of man. It was noted how the sin of the first man brought the whole human race into sin and ruin. We are now ready to look at the doctrine of sin in a little more detail.

The **Baptist Faith and Message** does not have a separate article on sin. It does acknowledge that all men are sinners, and that "only the grace of God can bring man into His holy fellowship" (Art. III). However, sin is a significant biblical doctrine and needs a little more elaboration. In this study we will deal with the origin and nature of sin.

## Origin

The absolute origin of sin is a deep mystery which is not open to the full understanding of man. The purpose of the Genesis narrative is not to give an account of the origin of sin in the universe. It is concerned only with how it began in the human race. Sin was already in the world, as the existence of the tempter in Genesis 3 plainly testifies. Therefore, the origin of sin must have preceded the creation and fall of man.

While there are no full biblical statements on the subject, enough information is given to form a rather clear picture. There is a definite indication that before sin entered the human race, another order of created beings had already sinned against God. The Bible assumes that Satan is the chief and head of these heavenly creatures who sinned. Originally they were created good; however, endowed with the power of choice, they deliberately chose to corrupt their holy character and rebel against their creator (cf. Jude 6; II Pe. 2:4; I Tim. 3:6; Isa. 14: 12-14; Ezek. 28: 1-19).

While this picture is clear enough in the Bible, there is still a great mystery connected with the origin of evil. For instance, we are not told why God permitted sin to begin in his universe. Much speculation has been made concerning this question, but the biblical writers were content to let the answer remain among the hidden secrets of God. One thing, however, is clear. While God no doubt could have prevented sin, he is never to be regarded as the author of sin. Sin originated in a deliberate act of free will on the part of some of God's creatures.

## Nature of Sin

With this in mind, we are able to see something of the nature of sin. Basically, sin is rebellion. It is a willful disobedience to the divine will on the part of responsible creatures. It may be defined more fully with the following three summary statements:

First, sin is something we are. That is, sin exists in man's mind and heart. It is an inward corruption of man's nature. It is this state or condition of man's moral nature which causes him to commit overt acts of sin (cf. Jer. 17:9; Mk. 7:21-23; Eph. 2:3).

Second, sin is something we do. That is, the sinful nature of man inevitably results in sinful acts. John defines sin as "the transgression of the law" (I Jn. 3:4). The law, of course, is the divine law. The Ten Commandments constitute a brief summary of this law. Thus, if anyone doubts that he has sinned, let him compare his conduct with the Ten Commandments. To break even one makes man a sinner (Gal. 3:10; Ja. 2:9-11).

Third, sin is not only something we do, it is also something we fail to do. It is a falling short (Rom. 3:23). The basic meaning of the most frequently used words for sin in the Old Testament and New Testament means "missing the mark." The mark which the sinner misses is God's righteousness. Thus, sin is not only the transgression of God's holy law, it is also the corruption of the holy character which God originally imparted to man.

Sin, then, may be defined in the following manner: It is an ideal we fail to reach, and a violation of God's holy law. Thus, sin is anything in man which does not express, or which is contrary to the holy character of God.


## 30. THE CONSEQUENCES OF SIN

The Bible takes sin very seriously. As we have seen, it views sin as rebellion against God. It is a revolution in the spirit-realm, and its ultimate aim is to usurp the sovereign authority of God. Therefore, every sin, even the smallest, is of greatest significance, and thus has serious consequences. What are these consequences?

### Guilt
First, sin brings guilt. By this we do not mean that it simply makes man feel bad. To be sure, sin does affect man's conscience, and, unless hardened, gives him feelings of shame and fear. However, guilt itself must not be confused with "guilt feelings". Guilt may be defined as that consequence of sin which makes the sinner worthy of punishment for his sin. Sin makes the sinner guilty whether he feels like it or not (Rom. 3:19). In other words, man is answerable and accountable to God for his sins. This springs from the fact that sin is a deliberate, responsible act (cf. Rom. 1:18, 21, 28, 32).

### Punishment
Second, since sin brings guilt, it also brings punishment. Since the Bible views sin as a responsible, deliberate act, it consequently views sin as deserving punishment. The punishment for sin is summed up in the Bible with the word death. God told Adam if he disobeyed he would die (Gen. 2:17). God said through the prophet Ezekial that "the soul that sinneth shall die" (Ez. 18:4, 20). The New Testament witness is the same (Rom. 5: 12-14; I Cor. 15: 21-22; Rom. 6:23; Ja. 1: 15).

The death penalty for sin includes physical death (Gen. 3:19), spiritual death (Eph. 2:1, 5), and finally eternal death (Rev. 20: 14). Physical death needs no explanation, but the other two kinds may need further comment. Spiritual death is that result of sin which separates man from the life of God (Eph. 4:18). It is the severance of the soul from God, its only life.

Eternal death may be looked upon as an endless extension of spiritual death. The Bible refers to it as the "second death" (Rev. 20:6, 14; 21:8). It involves the forfeiture of eternal life (Jn. 3:36; I Jn. 5:12), which is the irrevocable banishment of the body and soul from God's presence (II Thes. 1:9). This eternal spiritual death is without doubt the most serious consequence of sin.

The seriousness with which the Bible views sin stands in great contrast to the light views of sin held by many in this day. The Bible says that "fools make a mock at sin" (Prov. 14:9), and we seem to have an extraordinarily large number who fit that description today. There is probably no subject which has received more scorn, sarcasm, and derision. Sin is quite frequently dismissed, ignored, joked about, denied, and even glorified. Few attempt to take it seriously.

The tendency in modern views of sin is to take the blame from man and place it upon his economic conditions, his home life, his environment, or his biological makeup. The sinner is thus not to be blamed and punished; he is only to be   pitied. The Bible, on the other hand, will not permit us to be so deceived. The sinner is a responsible individual who will one day have to face God's righteous judgment.

# Part VI

## THE DOCTRINE OF SALVATION

# 31. GOD'S METHOD OF SAVING MEN

The past several articles in this series have been devoted to man and sin. These studies have revealed that man needs to be saved, and that it is impossible for him to save himself. Sin has brought him under guilt and condemnation. Sin has separated man from God and made it impossible for God to bless him. God's holy nature demands that He punish the sinner and his sins.

What can man do about this situation? Nothing! Man is in debt to God, and he has nothing with which to pay. Man needs his sins taken away, but he cannot atone for them nor undo his past misdeeds. Man needs a new nature, but he cannot regenerate himself. Sin has so infected man's total being that it is impossible for him to use any of his faculties to redeem himself.

What hope, then, is there for man's salvation? This is what the gospel is all about. It is the good news of God's salvation for man. What man cannot do for himself, God has done for him through Christ (Rom. 5:7). Paul gives a summary description of God's method of saving men in Romans 3: 20-31. After demonstrating that man needs to be saved, and showing the utter impossibility of saving himself, he proceeds to describe God's method of salvation. It has the following features:

### Apart from Law
First, God's method of saving men is apart from the law (Rom. 3: 20-21). Man cannot achieve salvation by the keeping of the law. This is not because of any imperfection in the law. On the contrary, the law is holy, and just and good (Rom. 7:12). The reason why no person can be justified by the law is because of man's weakness, his inability to keep it (Rom. 8:3). Thus, if man is to be saved, a righteousness must be provided for him without the law. This God has done (Rom. 3:21).

### By Faith
Second, God's method of saving man is "by faith of Jesus Christ" (Rom. 3:22). That is, the manner by which righteousness is attained is through faith. God demands righteousness of men. His justice and holiness demands that all unrighteousness be punished. Man is unrighteous. He is powerless to attain righteousness by keeping the law. However, while the righteousness demanded by God cannot be **achieved** by keeping the law, it may be **received** by faith.

### Free
Thus, in the third place, God's salvation for men is free. The phrase "justified freely by his grace" (Rom. 3: 24) expresses in

emphatic terms the freeness of God's salvation. Though the words "freely" and "grace" are not the same, they express the same ideas. Both contain the ideas of the freeness of the gift and the undeservedness of the receiver of the gift. The expression is, then, simply intended to express in the strongest way possible the absolute freeness of salvation. It is all of God, and nothing in God's saving act belongs to, or proceeds from man. It is absolutely without cost.

### Based on Christ's Death

Finally, God's method of saving men is based on the death of Christ. Several expressions in this summary description connect salvation with Christ's death. The words "redemption," "propitiation", and "blood" all point to the sacrifice which Christ made for man's salvation. It is through Christ's death that our salvation is made possible, for in his death Christ paid the penalty for man's sin (II Cor. 5:21; Heb. 2:9). More on this in the next study.

## 32. SALVATION PROVIDED: THE ATONEMENT

The atonement is the central doctrine of Christianity. It is feared, however, that the doctrine is so little emphasized today that many do not know the meaning of the word nor what the doctrine is all about. If one divides the term into three words he has AT-ONE-MENT. It means reconciliation, agreement, concord. In one passage it is used to translate the Greek word for reconciliation (Rom. 5:11).

The doctrine of the atonement, therefore, deals with how God and man become reconciled. We have seen in past studies that sin has separated man from God. Thus, man in his sins is at enmity against God (Rom. 8:7), and God has a controversy with man (Rom. 1:18). How can a sinful man and a holy God be reconciled? This is what the doctrine of the atonement is all about.

Reconciliation between God and man is based on the death of Christ. So, in reality, the doctrine of the atonement is the same as the doctrine of Christ's death. It deals particularly with the significance and purpose of his death.

There can be little doubt that the death of Christ is the central feature of the entire Biblical revelation. It is the theme of the Old Testament (Lk. 24:25-27). It was prefigured in the sacrificial system (Heb. 9:22-28), and predicted by the prophets (Isa. 53). It was the central theme of Jesus' teaching about his primary mission (Mt. 26:53-54; Mk. 8:31; Lk. 12:50; Jn. 12:27-28). It was the central theme of the preaching and writings of the apostles (Acts 2:23; I Cor. 2:1-2; 15:1-4).

The prominence of Christ's death cannot be doubted, but what is its meaning? Why did Christ die? This is a very important question and every Christian needs to have a firm understanding of the answer.

### Erroneous Views

First, it is necessary to point out some erroneous views of the death of Christ. One is that Christ died simply as a martyr. Another is that Christ died to give us an example to follow. Both of these views are related and view Christ's death in the same light as the death of other great men. His death is thus seen as a result of evil men and circumstances. It took place because he was not understood or because of his teaching or for political reasons. This explanation of Christ's death seems to have a strong appeal to many today.

There is some truth in these claims, of course. However, neither touches on the chief significance of Christ's death. Christ is not pictured in the Bible as the helpless victim of evil men and circumstances. His life was not taken from him; he gave it up (Jn. 10:15-18). Christ's death was in the redemptive plan and purpose of God before the foundation of the world (Acts 2:23; Rev. 13:8). Any adequate view of Christ's death must therefore include the following:

### Substitutionary

First, Christ's death must be related to man's sin. In this sense his death was substitutionary. He "died for our sins" (I Cor. 15:3). It must be emphasized that he died **for** our sins and not simply **because** of our sins. There is an important difference. In his death Christ became our sin-bearer (I Pe. 2:24). He was the innocent one dying for the guilty (II Cor. 5:21).

### Satisfaction

Second, Christ's death must be related to God's holiness. In this sense his death was a satisfaction. God's holiness and justice demanded that the full penalty for sin be paid. Therefore, God has a claim against the sinner which is impossible for the sinner to meet. The death of Christ fully met all these claims against the sinner. Thus Christ's work on the cross secured a satisfactory basis whereby sin may be forgiven and God still remains just and holy (Rom. 3:26).

The death of Christ becomes, then, the supreme demonstration of God's love and mercy and his holiness and wrath. The necessity of Christ's death demonstrates his holiness and hatred of sin; his willingness to give his son as the sinbearer demonstrates his love and mercy.

## 33. SALVATION APPLIED:
## ELECTION AND REGENERATION

The past several studies have dealt with man's need to be saved and God's provision for his salvation. The previous study dealt particularly with the atoning work of Christ. However, this work alone is not enough for man's salvation. The atoning work of Christ was primarily Godward; that is, it removed all obstacles in the way of God's pardon of the sinner. In other words, the death of Christ provided the basis by which the sinner may be forgiven of his sins.

However, the sinner in his natural state is opposed to God. He, therefore, must be brought to accept God's provision for his salvation, and must learn to love and serve God. In other words, the salvation which God has made possible must be applied to the individual sinner.

In the application of salvation there are two sides - the divine and the human. In bringing the sinner to accept his offer of salvation God works in perfect accordance with his own nature and also with that of man. This study is concerned with the divine side. It includes two things:

### Election

First, God decrees to save sinners. God has not only provided and offered a way for all sinners to escape the condemnation for sin, he has definitely planned to bring some to accept this salvation. This purpose of God to save is called election.

Election is not an easy concept to understand nor accept by a great many people. The term itself simply means choice. With reference to God's part in saving sinners it means that God has decreed to bring certain ones, upon whom his heart has been eternally set, to faith in Christ as Saviour. Thus, God plans to save sinners, and he chooses those who shall be saved. This choice is clearly God's and not man's for it was made "before the foundation of the world." (Eph. 1:4).

However difficult election may be to understand and regardless of the problems it poses, it must be recognized that it is a biblical teaching (ch. Mt. 24:22; 25:34; Lk. 18:7; Jn. 6:37, 44:17:2, 6; Acts 13:48; Rom. 8:27-30; 9:11-16; Eph. 1:5-8; Col. 3:12; 2 Thes. 2:13; I Pe. 1:12). It is also a historical Baptist doctrine. The **Baptist Faith and Message** affirms the doctrine. (Art. V) It is even more strongly affirmed in older Baptist statements of faith. One may find the doctrine affirmed and explained in more detail by the Baptist writers, J. P. Boyce, **Abstract of Theology**, pp. 302-328; E. C. Dargan, **The Doctrine of Our Faith**, pp. 143-144; and W.T. Conner, **Christian Doctrine**, pp. 153-156.

### Regeneration

Second, God not only plans to bring sinners to salvation, he acts upon the souls of those whom he has chosen to save. God so acts upon the heart of man that his rebellious nature is changed. This work of God in salvation is expressed principally by the word regeneration.

Regeneration is defined in the **Baptist Faith and Message** as "a work of God's grace whereby believers become new creatures in Christ Jesus. It is a change of heart wrought by the Holy Spirit through conviction of sin, to which the sinner responds in repentance toward God and faith in the Lord Jesus Christ" (Art. IV, A). It should be noted that it is "a work of God's grace." It is a divine work and not a human change of heart. It is a creative act of God's Spirit in the sinner's heart (Jn. 1:13; 3:3, 5).

Regeneration effects a change in the sinner's disposition. The prevailing disposition of the unregenerate soul is opposed to God. In regeneration this opposition is changed to love and loyalty. There is a reversal of the natural sinful disposition, and after regeneration the controlling principle is love and loyalty to God (II Cor. 5:17).

Thus, God's work in salvation is electing and regenerating. In the next study we will look at man's part.


## 34. SALVATION APPLIED: CONVERSION

It was noted in the last study that there is both a divine and a human element in the application of the saving work of Christ to the sinner. It was seen that God's work is that of electing and regenerating. But man also has an important part to perform in the application of salvation.

It must be stressed that man's part is necessary. The fact that God elects those whom he will save and regenerates them in no way rules out the necessity of man's activity. If man is to be saved he must be actively involved in his salvation.

Man's part in his salvation is summed up in the act of conversion. In one sense conversion is also an act of God (I Kgs. 18:37; Psa. 80:3; Jer. 31:18). However, it is primarily an act in which man willingly cooperates with God. Conversion, seen as a willing activity of man, comprises two essential acts-repentance and faith.

## Repentance

First, conversion includes the act of repentance. Repentance basically means to change one's view, mind, or purpose. It necessarily implies the disapproval and abandonment of past opinions and purposes, and the acceptance of others which are different. In its full meaning the scriptural view of repentance involves three elements:

(1) A change of mind. Repentance is something a person thinks. Before repentance the sinner delights in his sins and takes no thought of God. But the time comes when there is a change. He views his relationship to sin and God differently. He changes his mind toward these things.

(2) A change of feeling. Repentance is something we feel. It consists in feeling one is a sinner in God's sight, and feeling genuine sorrow for this condition. The intensity of feeling will vary in individuals, but the emotional element in repentance is essential. It is impossible to really change one's mind about a thing without having a corresponding change of feeling.

(3) A change of will. Repentance is something we do. If we change our minds about a matter, and the feelings are strong enough, there will follow a change of action. This is the true test of genuine repentance. If the change in mind about sin and the emotional sorrow for sin does not result in a turning from sin, it cannot be called scriptural repentance.

## Faith

The second act in conversion is faith. Faith is a great word in the Bible with a rich content. It is the aspect of conversion in which the sinner turns to Christ for salvation. It is the means by which God's provision for salvation is made a reality in the individual's experience. Like repentance it includes three elements:

(1) The intellectual element. Faith includes an intellectual acceptance of the truth that Jesus is the Saviour. This involves a knowledge of the essential facts of the gospel (Rom. 10:14-17).

(2) The emotional element. Intellectual assent to the facts of Christ is not enough to constitute saving faith. There must be a deep feeling that these facts are significant and personal. This aspect of faith we may call trust or confidence in Christ. It is a willingness to commit ourselves to him.

(3) The volitional element. Faith also involves an act of the will. It is a wilful act of submission to Christ as Lord (Rom. 10:9).

Conversion, then, consists of the two acts of repentance and faith. Both are necessary to have genuine conversion. They are the two sides to the same coin. One cannot really exist without the other.

One is a turning from sin, the other is a turning to Christ as the only solution for sin. Both are necessary if man is to be saved.

## 35. THE NEW RELATION BETWEEN GOD AND MAN

Our study of salvation has brought us to consider the new relationship between God and man. In past studies we have looked at man's need to be saved, God's provision for salvation, God's work in bringing man to accept his provision, and man's part in responding. We now turn to consider the new relation between God and man which grows out of his acceptance by faith of God's provision and offer of salvation.

The Scriptures represent the new relation between God and man in several different ways. This new relationship is so manifold, so rich and full, that no one term can express the completeness of it. Here we will consider three terms which the New Testament uses to describe what happens between God and man in salvation. These terms not only describe the new relation but also tell us something about the condition of man before salvation.

### Justification
The first term is **justification** (Rom. 3:24, 26, 28; I Cor. 6:7-8). Justification is considered by many to be the greatest article of Christian doctrine. Unfortunately, the term is not used very frequently today and consequently many Christians do not know its meaning.

Justification is a legal term. It comes from the law courts of the Roman world. It means to declare not guilty, innocent or righteous. It is similar to our word acquittal. With reference to salvation it refers to God's gracious act by which he declares the guilty sinner not guilty and accepts him and treats him as righteous.

Justification, thus, describes the sinner as a law-breaker, a criminal. This may seem harsh language, but it is scriptural teaching (I Jn. 3:4). Before salvation we were under judgment, the just sentence of God (Jn. 3:18). Through faith in Christ this is changed. We now have a new legal standing with God. We are justified.

### Adoption
The second term is **adoption** (Eph. 1:5). Adoption is a well-known practice which has existed in human society for a long time. It is the procedure by which one takes a child who is not naturally his own and makes him so legally with all the rights of a real child. With reference to salvation it refers to the act by which God chooses to

70

take those who are not his children, and make them such by adopting them into his family.

Adoption tells us that before salvation no one is a child of God. The Bible knows nothing of the popularly held notion of the brotherhood of man and the fatherhood of God. Before salvation we are "children of wrath" (Eph. 2:2) and "children of the devil" (I Jn. 3:10; Jn. 8:44). In salvation, however, the relation is changed. We are declared sons of God with the full inheritance of a son (Rom. 8:17; Rev. 21:7).

### Reconciliation

The third term is **reconciliation** (Rom. 5:10; 2 Cor. 5:18). The English word "reconcile" means to make friendly again or to win over to a friendly attitude. The Greek word has a very similar meaning. It was the characteristic word which described the bringing together again people who have been estranged.

Reconciliation describes the sinner before salvation as an enemy of God. Man was made for friendship and fellowship with God. However, through man's sin of disobedience and rebellion he is now at enmity with God (Rom. 5:10). In salvation this enmity is taken away. Man and God are no longer enemies but friends (Jn. 15:15). "Ye are no more strangers and foreigners, but ye are fellow citizens with the saints, and of the household of God" (Eph. 2:19).


## 36. THE FINAL PERSERVERANCE OF THE SAINTS

Any treatment of the doctrines of salvation must include some discussion of the perseverance of the believer in salvation. This doctrine is sometimes popularly called "once saved always saved" and the "eternal security of the believer." It is a well-known, historic and cherished belief of Baptists. The **Baptist Faith and Message** states the doctrine as follows:

"All true believers endure to the end. Those whom God has accepted in Christ, and sanctified by His Spirit, will never fall away from the state of grace, but shall persevere to the end. Believers may fall into sin through neglect and temptation, whereby they grieve the Spirit, impair their graces and comforts, bring reproach on the cause of Christ, and temporal judgments on themselves, yet they shall be kept by the power of God through faith unto salvation" (Art. V).

Many other Christians hold this belief in common with Baptists. Many Christians also disagree with Baptists on this matter. The doctrine is often misrepresented by those who hold it and misunderstood by those who reject it. It is important, therefore, that we have a firm grasp as to what the doctrine is all about.

71

## Meaning

It may be helpful, first of all, to emphasize what the doctrine does not mean or imply. It does not mean that a believer will never sin. As the **Baptist Faith and Message** explains: "Believers may fall into sin through neglect and temptation..." On the other hand, the doctrine does not mean that a person will be saved regardless of what he is or does.

What then does the doctrine teach? It simply means that God will cause those who truly believe in Jesus to persevere to the end. It asserts that the regenerating grace of God so changes a person that he can never be the same again. It is not that a Christian will be saved whether he continues in faith and holiness or not. Indeed, the doctrine teaches that no one will be saved unless he perseveres. However, it further teaches that the enabling grace of God will cause the believer to continue in faith and godliness and thus attain final salvation. If he does not continue in faith and holiness he is not a true believer (I Jn. 2:19). In other words, the saints will persevere because God preserves them (I Pe. 1:5).

## Biblical Evidence

The biblical evidence for the doctrine of perseverance is plain and abundant. All of it cannot be presented here. We will content ourselves with the following statements of proof:

First, it is proven by the manner in which we are saved. Salvation is by grace through faith (Eph. 2:8-9). We do not work to get salvation, nor can we work to keep it. In other words, God does not bring us into a saving relationship by faith and then put us on the basis of works and from there on we must work to keep it. Salvation is by faith from beginning to end (Gal. 3:1-5).

Second, it is proved by what God does for us in salvation. He gives us **eternal** life (Jn. 3:15-16; 5:24). He seals us with the Holy Spirit until the day of redemption (Eph. 1:13; 4:30). He makes us children of God (Gal. 3:26; I Jn. 3:1-2). He brings us into a vital relationship with Christ so that he dwells in us and we in him (Jn. 14:20; I Jn. 3:24). All these descriptions of salvation are particularly related to the assurance that what God began in us at salvation he will finish (Phil. 1:6; I Cor. 1:8-9).

Third, it is proven by what Christ is doing for the believer now. Christ is making intercession for every believer now. Because of this intercession Christ is able to save completely, to the end (Heb. 7:25). This fact that Jesus is now living and active on the believer's behalf is a solid basis for his safety.

Fourth, it is proven by the many direct scriptural references to the doctrine. To list all of them would be to transcribe a large portion of the Bible. There are the many promises of God's faithfulness (Psa. 37: 24-48; Isa. 55: 3; Jer. 32:40). There are the many references in the New Testament which cannot be explained on any other basis (Jn. 10: 28-29; Rom. 8: 35-39; I Pe. 1: 3-5; 2 Thes. 3:3; I Cor. 1:8-9). The reader will be greatly blessed by reading all these references and carefully studying them.

# Part VII

# THE DOCTRINE OF THE CHRISTIAN LIFE

## 37. THE CHRISTIAN LIFE:
## ITS CONTEMPLATIVE SIDE

The Christian experience does not end with the salvation experience. The saving act is only the beginning. There is a life to be lived after salvation. This life is a continuation of the saving act of faith. This we will call the doctrine of the Christian life.

The Christian life has two sides to it. There is the contemplative side, and there is the active side. The one consists of prayer, meditation, Bible study, and such like; the other consists of work. In order to have a healthy Christian life, both of these sides are necessary.

In this study we will look at the contemplative side. This is sometimes called the devotional life of the Christian. This aspect of the Christian life is often discounted, but it should not be. The contemplative elements are some of the most necessary and important parts of the Christian life. In fact, if the active or work part of the Christian life In fact, if the active or work part of the Christian life is to be effective and fulfilling it must be preceeded by the contemplative. It could very well be that the reason why many Christians are doing more "Christian works" and enjoying it less is because they have neglected the source of power and strength for Christian activity. This comes through the contemplative side of Christianity, which consists of two essential elements.

### Prayer

First, there is prayer. Through his example and direct teaching Jesus has taught us the importance of prayer. On a number of occasions he found it necessary to withdraw from his activities to pray (Lk. 6:12; 9:18; 11:1). In his teaching he bids us and encourages us to pray (Mt. 5:6; Lk. 18:1ff.)

Elsewhere in the Scriptures we are taught the need and importance of prayer. To fail to pray is sin (I Sam. 12:23). The apostles regarded prayer as one of the most important things that could engage their time or attention (Acts 6:4). Prayer was a characteristic feature of Paul's life (Rom. 1:9; I Thes. 1:2), and he urges all believers to continue in prayer (Col. 4:2; I Thes. 5:17). James actually tells us that we may lack the necessary blessings of life because of a failure to pray (Ja. 4:2).

A study of prayer in the Bible reveals that true prayer consists of many elements. It includes adoration, communion, thanksgiving, intercession, confession, and petition, to name some of them. An examination of the Model Prayer (commonly called the Lord's Prayer), will reveal all these elements.

Many Christians find prayer to be one of the most difficult things to do. Many books have been written giving instructions on how to pray, and some of them are very helpful. However, it is very difficult for one person to tell another how to pray. Jesus is our best teacher at this point. The best thing to do is just pray. It will take determination and discipline but the rewards are worth it.

### Bible Study

The second element in the contemplative side of the Christian life is the reading of the scriptures. This is another basic and vital element in the Christian life, but one which is widely neglected. Most Christians have been told about the importance of Bible study, but it seems to always be escaping us.

The Scriptures themselves point out the necessity of studying the Holy Scriptures in order to have a strong Christian life. The Psalmist stated that it was through the meditation in the law that brought happiness because it brought strength, stability, and productivity to the reader (Psa. 1). The word of God has a cleansing effect on those who heed it (Psa. 119:9), it gives strength to resist temptation (Psa. 119:11), and provides direction for all who will read it (Psa. 119:105). It makes us "wise unto salvation" (II Tim. 3:15), and makes for strong, mature spiritual lives.

Prayer and Bible study seem so elementary for these days in which so much needs to be done. Neither, however, is a Mickey Mouse affair. Both are absolutely necessary if we are to live the Christian life as it ought to be lived.

In the next study we will look at the active side of the Christian life.

## 38. THE MISSION AND WORK OF THE CHRISTIAN

There are two sides to the Christian life--the contemplative and the active. In the last study we discussed the contemplative side. We now take up the active side. To discuss in full all that is involved here would take several installments. Thus, we will consider only two essential aspects of the active side of the Christian life.

### Witness

The first of these aspects has to do with evangelism. Every Christian should be a witness for Christ. That is, he should be actively engaged in bringing others into a saving relationship with Christ. In light of the New Testament teaching this must be considered one of the most important of all Christian activites.

We are taught by both precept and example in the New Testament to be witnesses. The last words Jesus left us were words instructing us in this mission (Mt. 28: 19-20; Mk. 16:15; Jn. 20:21; Acts 1:8). The early disciples understood this to be the responsibility of every Christian, and not simply the task of a specialized group (Acts 8:4).

But not only are we expressly and repeatedly commanded to be witnesses, there seems to be an inborn desire in every Christian to be a witness. The new life which the Christian has received in Christ creates a spontaneous impulse to bring others to know the same Christ (Rom. 10:1). As the **Baptist Faith and Message** puts it: "The new birth of man's spirit by God's Holy Spirit means the birth of love for others" (Art. XI). Sometimes this impulse is not cultivated, and as a consequence many Christians lose this sense of mission. When this happens a stunted and degenerated form of the Christian life results.

### Good Works

The second aspect of the active side of the Christian life is in the area of good works. Some have referred to this aspect of Christian activity as social action. It has to do with doing good toward others.

It is plain in the Bible that good works are expected from the Christian life (Eph. 2:10; Tit. 1:16; 2:7-14). Indeed, good works are considered to be the natural result of a genuine Christian experience. If good works do not follow, then the experience is suspect (Mt. 7:15-20; Ja. 1: 17-26).

The activity of the Christian in the area of good works is a broad area. As we have opportunity we are to do good to all men (Gal. 6:10). This includes a wide scope of deeds and relationships with people. The Christian should work to provide for the orphans and widows (Ja. 1:27; Isa. 1:17). He is to care for the needy (Rom. 12:13), the aged (I Tim. 5:9-10), the helpless (Mt. 25: 31-46), and the sick (Mt. 25:36; Ja. 5:14). Good works include such simple matters as hospitality (Rom. 12:13), courtesy (Eph. 4:32), and generosity in sharing our material blessings (Acts 20:35).

In this matter of good works a word of caution needs to be given. Good works must never degenerate into a works salvation. Works are never to be performed in order to earn a good standing with God. We must ever keep in mind that works are to issue from a right standing with God and a new life in Christ. Works should be motivated by a genuine love for God who has saved us, and not by the thought that we can somehow earn his favor and love.

Another thing to keep in mind is that not all works are necessarily spiritual or Christian activity. When works are performed for some selfish motive they are not Christian works. Good works are never to be an end in themselves. They are always to be done to bring glory to our Heavenly Father (Mt. 5:16).

When then are works truly Christian? When they are done according to God's revealed will in the scriptures, out of a heart of love for God, and in the power of the Holy Spirit (cf. Rom. 14:17-18; Gal. 5:22-26).

## 39. DOCTRINE OF SANCTIFICATION

Sanctification is an aspect of God's saving work which has been too long neglected in Baptist life. Perhaps it is because some groups have associated it with sinless perfection or a "second blessing." Whatever the reasons, the neglect of this important doctrine is unjustified. Sanctification is a biblical word and a significant element in God's plan of salvation for the believer.

### The Meaning

The word "sanctify" has two related meanings in the Bible. Basically the term means to set apart some object from a common use to a sacred one, such as the seventh day (Gen. 2:3), the tabernacle (Ex. 29:44), and the temple (2 Chr. 29:5). Thus the basic idea in sanctification is that of separateness. But "sanctify" is also used in a moral sense, meaning "to make holy". This meaning is quite naturally based on the original idea of separateness. The "sanctified" object or person is separated unto God, and like God, is to be holy (I Pet. 1:16).

The Christian doctrine of sanctification is concerned primarily with the second idea of making holy or pure. When a person is regenerated he is given a new nature, a holy disposition. Sanctification is concerned with the maintaining, strengthening, and development of that holy disposition given in the new birth.

### The Process of Sanctification

The New Testament presents the process of sanctification in a two-fold light. In one sense every believer is sanctified (I Cor. 6:11). It happened at the moment of regeneration. When a person is born again, the Holy Spirit consecrates him to God by indwelling him and making his body His temple (I Cor. 6:19). Thus the believer is already "sanctified in Christ Jesus" (I Cor. 1:2). He is a "saint", one of the "holy brethren" (Heb. 3:1), and because of this sanctification he is called upon to live a holy life.

In another sense, however, sanctification is presented as something incomplete which needs to be developed. Sanctification is incomplete in that the "flesh" principle is not removed at regeneration, and in that the new Christian is a babe in Christ and needs to grow in grace. Therefore, the Christian is admonished to "put off the old man" and "put on the new man". He is to cleanse himself "from all filthiness of the flesh and spirit, perfecting holiness in the fear of God" (2 Cor. 7:1).

## The Means of Sanctification

The means through which sanctification is wrought in the believer is the indwelling Spirit of Christ. To enable the believer to progress in sanctification the Spirit renews him daily (2 Cor. 4:16). It is important to remember at this point that, like justification, sanctification is not produced by the works of the law or the works of the flesh (Gal. 3:3). Christ is our sanctification (I Cor. 1:30) and it is the work of the Spirit to produce in us Christlikeness (Gal. 5:22-23). Thus in order to progress in sanctification, we must "walk in the Spirit" (Gal. 5:16).

## The Goal of Sanctification

The goal of sanctification is nothing short of perfect Christian character - to be like Jesus. God wants us to be completely sanctified in body, soul, and spirit (I Thes. 5:23). That this goal is not attainable in this life is clearly demonstrated by the teaching of Scripture and experience (cf. Phil 3:13-21; Col. 3:4; I Jn. 3:2). Yet the Christian is admonished to hunger and thirst for righteousness (Matt. 5:6), to press toward the mark of Christian perfectness (Phil. 3:14), and to seek to be conformed to the image of Christ (Rom. 12:2).


## 40. CHRISTIAN ASSURANCE

Is it possible for one to know that he is saved? According to the Bible it is not only possible, but one should have this assurance. We are admonished to make our "calling and election sure" (2 Pe. 1:10). One book of the New Testament was written for this purpose (I Jn. 5:13). To know that one has been accepted by God is what W. T. Conner calls the "normal Christian experience" (**Christian Doctrine**, p. 219).

### Nature of Christian Assurance

Christian assurance is the conscious awareness that one has been accepted by God. It is a personal, experiential relationship with God. In the salvation experience one comes to know God (Jn. 17:3; II Tim. 1:12), and to be known by God (Gal. 4:9). Salvation in the Christian sense is a conscious transaction. We are conscious that our sins have been forgiven and that we have entered into fellowship with God (I Jn. 1:3). Christian assurance understood as a conscious relationship with God is characterized by several elements. Joy, peace, love, and hope result from this new relationship with God (Acts 8:8; 13:52; Rom. 5:1, 5; 8:24).

## Loss of Assurance

Some feel that if a person is really saved he will always know it. However, both the New Testament and Christian experience indicate that it is possible to be genuinely saved but still have no clear and definite consciousness of ones acceptance with God. John's first epistle was written so that those who believe might know that they have eternal life (I Jn. 5:13). This clearly implies that a person might be a genuine believer but for some reason be made to doubt his salvation. If this were not so then the primary purpose for I John is meaningless.

There are a number of reasons why a person might not be sure of his salvation. It is possible to be confused by false teachers (cf. Gal. 1:7; I Jn. 2:26). Sin will break our fellowship with God and rob us of assurance (I Jn. 1:7). Sometimes a lack of assurance results from an inadequate understanding of the ground of our forgiveness in the atoning work of Christ (cf. Gal. 3:1-3).

## Way to Assurance

If a person lacks assurance, how does he obtain it? The following suggestions may be helpful:

First, assurance comes by way of knowledge. "Faith cometh by hearing", the Bible says (Rom. 10:17). In order to have assurance one needs a knowledge and understanding of the fundamental things in salvation. Especially does he need to know that Christ has made full provision for our sins and that we are saved through faith.

Second, assurance may be gained through examination. Peter tells us we are to make our "calling and election sure" (2 Pe. 1:10). John tells us how we may do this. In his first epistle he lays down three tests which we should apply to our Christian experience to see if it is genuine. (1) There is the moral test. Are we trying to obey Christ (I Jn. 2:3-6)? (2) There is the social test. Do we love our fellowman (I Jn. 2:9-11; 4:7 ff.)? (3) There is the doctrinal test. Do we believe that Jesus is the Christ (I Jn. 5:1ff.)?

Third, assurance comes through surrender to Christ as Lord. We must hold nothing back. Deliberate and willful disobedience usually brings doubt about ones relationship to God. Complete surrender brings assurance (cf. Jn. 7:17).

Part VIII


# THE DOCTRINE OF THE CHURCH

# 41. THE NATURE OF THE CHURCH (Part I)

After a person is saved he not only has an individual Christian life to live, he also has a life to live in common with others. This corporate Christian life we will discuss under the doctrine of the church. The particular aspect of the church which we will start with in this study has to do with its nature. What is a New Testament church?

There are many false notions as to what a church is today. Perhaps one of the most common misunderstandings is to identify the church with a building, or a meeting place. Others have mistakenly understood the church as an invisible, universal mass of all believers, both living and dead. Some have identified it with the spiritual kingdom of God on earth.

The **Baptist Faith and Message** defines a New Testament church as "a local body of baptized believers who are associated by covenant in the faith and fellowship of the gospel, observing the two ordinances of Christ, committed to His teachings, exercising the gifts, rights, and privileges invested in them by His Word, and seeking to extend the gospel to the ends of the earth" (Art. VI).

The above definition is a familiar one to most informed Baptists. It has been defined by Baptists in essentially this same manner ever since we have been drawing up statements of faith. There are a number of essential elements in this definition, all of which are necessary to define what the New Testament teaches about the nature of a gospel church.

## A Local Body

First, a New Testament church is a local group of believers. The word for "church" is used 114 times in the New Testament. Five of these occurrences have no reference to the New Testament church, leaving a total of 109 references to Christian assemblies. Of these 109 references the great majority refer to a local congregation of believers. Some scholars feel that "church" is never used in the New Testament in any other sense but that of a local assembly.

A number of times "church" is used in the singular to refer to a specific church, as that of Thessalonica (I Thess. 1:1; cf. I Cor. 1:2). The word is used in the plural to refer to a group of churches in a particular region (Gal. 1: 22). It is never used to designate a national or international body or organization. Dr. W.T. Conner states it rather bluntly: "The only ecclesiastical organization found in the New Testament was that of a local church (**Christian Doctrine**, p. 259).

For this reason Baptist do not speak of "The Baptist Church" or "The Southern Baptist Church." We speak of churches. Churches may be associated together in conventions or associations, but the churches in these conventions and associations together do not form a church or "The Baptist Church".

## Visible

A second emphasis in this definition is that the church is a **body** or **company** of believers. This means that a New Testament church has a visibility. The Greek work translated "church" in the New Testament is **ekklesia**. It originally meant an assembly of people who were called together to consider matters of public interest. When our Lord and the Apostles used this word to describe His church they intended to describe a visible group of people gathered together for a specific purpose. Thus, the New Testament knows nothing of a nebulous, indefinable, invisible, scattered church. It only knows a church which has regular meetings (I Cor. 5: 4; 11: 19; 33-34; 14:19; Heb. 9:25), prescribed officers (I Tim. 3: 1-13; Eph. 4: 8-11), observes tangible ordinances (I Cor. 11: 23-34), and disciplines its members (I Cor. 5:4; Mt. 18: 15-17).

## 42. THE NATURE OF THE CHURCH (Part II)

The last study was the beginning of a discussion of the nature of a gospel church. Two characteristics were discussed--a New Testament church is **local** and **visible**. In this study we continue with this aspect of the church by looking at some more characteristics of a New Testament church.

### Believers

In addition to describing the church as local and visible, a third characteristic is that a New Testament church is a local, visible body of **believers**. A church is not simply a conglomerate or assembly of people. It is an assembly of people who believe in Jesus Christ as Saviour and Lord.

That a New Testament church is composed only of believers is amply demonstrated in the Scriptures. It is plainly stated that the first church was made up of those "that glady received His word" (Acts 2:41), those "that believe" (Acts 2:44), and those "who are saved" (Acts 2:47).

When Paul writes the churches he addresses them as "the called of Jesus Christ" (Rom. 1:6), "them that are sanctified in Christ Jesus" and who "call upon the name of Jesus Christ our Lord" (I Cor. 1:2). He calls them "saints" (I Cor. 1: 2; Eph. 1:1), the "faithful in Christ Jesus" (Eph. 1: 1), "the faithful brethren in Christ" (Col. 1: 2). All of these expressions indicate that the churches of the

New Testament were made up only of people who believed in Jesus as Saviour and Lord.

## Baptized Believers

But not only is a church made up of believers, a fourth characteristic is that it is made up of **baptized** believers. It is true that none but believers make up a true church. But not every company or group of believers constitute a church. They must be baptized believers.

The New Testament knows nothing of unbaptized church members. The idea is simply never entertained. The Book of Acts demonstrates that baptism was a universal practice in the New Testament churches, beginning at Pentecost (Acts 2: 38, 41) and continuing throughout the Apostolic period (cf. 8:12, 36-38; 9: 18; 10: 47; 16: 14-15, 33: 18:8; 19: 5). Even before this John the Baptist apparently baptized all who sincerely confessed their sins (Mk. 1: 5). Jesus and his disciples did the same (Jn. 3:22, 26; 4: 1-2). And our Lord commanded each convert to be baptized (Mt. 28: 19-20).

## Spiritual Organism

The fact that a church is made up of baptized believers in Jesus Christ implies a fifth important characteristic of a New Testament church. It is a **spiritual organism** and not merely an organization. A gospel church is made up of people who have been changed by the Spirit (I Cor. 6:11), indwelt by the Spirit (Rom. 8: 9), led by the Spirit (Rom. 8:14), and are brought together by the Spirit (Eph. 4: 3-4).

This all means that a New Testament church is a divine creation, a divine institution. It is not an organization on the order of a lodge or civic club. The church uniquely belongs to God. They are the "churches of Christ" (Rom. 16: 16), and the "churches of God" (I Th. 2: 14). As such, the members of the church are "God's elect" (Rom. 8: 33; Col. 3: 12). And being thus chosen and elected by God, the members of New Testament churches are "the people of God" (Rom. 9:25f.; I Pe. 2:10). The church owes its beginnings, its history, its present existence, and its destiny to the initiative and power of God's purpose and grace.


# 43. THE ORDINANCES: BAPTISM

Jesus committed certain rites or ceremonies to his churches which they are to observe and perpetuate until he comes again. These are called ordinances. Some people refer to them as "sacraments". Actually neither term is used in the New Testament to refer to these ceremonies, but since sacrament carries with it the idea of saving merit, Baptists have preferred to call them ordinances.

These ordinances which Christ left his churches are two and only two: baptism and the Lord's Supper. Since baptism comes first and is prerequisite to the Lord's Supper we will consider it first. We will discuss this ordinance around five points of emphasis.

### An Obligation

While the great majority of Christians agree that baptism is a definite obligation of every Christian, some deny that it is-namely, the Quakers. But the command of the Lord is plain on the matter (Mt. 28:19). Also Peter's exhortation leaves little doubt about the obligation (Acts 2:38). In addition to these definite commands, it is clear that the New Testament churches universally observed the ordinance of baptism (Acts 2:41; 8:12, 38; 9:18; 16:15, 33; 18:8; 19:5).

### The Mode

Christian baptism is the immersion of a believer in water. By immersion is meant the total submersion of a person in water, and, of course, raising him out again. That this is the New Testament mode of baptism is plainly indicated by the meaning of the word "baptize", and the descriptions of baptism recorded in the New Testament. Baptism comes from the Greek word **baptizo** which means to "dip under", "plunge", or "sink". All the descriptions of baptism in the New Testament are in keeping with this meaning (cf. Mk. 1:9-11; Jn. 3:23; Acts 8:38-39).

### The Subjects

Who should be baptized? The New Testament teaches that only believers are proper candidates for baptism. In the great commission Jesus states that we are first to make disciples and then baptize them (Mt. 28:19). The cases of baptism in the New Testament demonstrate that the New Testament churches followed this order. All the cases mentioned in the New Testament imply an act of belief and repentance, or some such personal experience which indicated conversion and profession of faith. The consistent pattern found in the New Testament is hearing and believing, and then being baptized (cf. Mk. 1:4-5; Jn. 4:1-2; Acts 2:41; 16-14, 15, 33-34).

### The Administrator

Who should baptize? One must admit that the New Testament is not as clear on this point as the others discussed here. However, there are two scriptural facts about baptism which cause us to conclude that the responsibility for administering the ordinance rests with the local church.

First, Christ's commission was given to the disciples as a group (Mt. 28:19-20). Baptism is not an ordinance which may be administered by an individual Christian simply at his own discretion. Even Peter had to get the approval of a delegation to baptize Cornelius and his household (Acts 10:47-48).

A second fact to note is that baptism is a means of publicly confessing Christ and identifying oneself with the local congregation of believers. If this is true, then baptism is not purely an individual act. It is a church ordinance and a church responsibility.

### The Design

What is the meaning of baptism? The teaching of scripture is that baptism is a symbol. Its purpose or design is not to save or help save. Its purpose is to symbolize or picture three things: (2) the believer's faith in a crucified, buried, and risen Saviour; (b) the believer's death to sin, the burial of the old life, and the resurrection to walk in newness of life in Christ; and (c) it expresses the hope of the final resurrection of the dead (Rom. 6:1-5; Col. 2:12).

## 44. THE ORDINANCES: THE LORD'S SUPPER

The second ordinance of the church is the Lord's Supper. This ordinance has also been called Holy Communion, the Eucharist, and the Mass. The biblical references to the ordinance refer to it as "the communion of the blood of Christ" and "the communion of the body of Christ" (I Cor. 10:16), "breaking of bread" (Acts 2:42; 20:7), the "Lord's table" (I Cor. 10:21), and the "Lord's Supper" (I Cor. 11:20). The "Lord's Supper" seems to be the most comprehensive designation, and it is the most commonly used term for the ordinance by Baptists (**Baptist Faith and Message**, Art. VII).

Many of the things said about baptism could also be said about the Lord's Supper. Here we will emphasize three things about the second ordinance.

### Its Institution

As in the case of baptism, it is clear that the Lord's Supper was instituted by Jesus himself. The account of the institution is recorded by the first three gospel writers (Mt. 26:26-29; Mk. 14:22-25; Lk. 22:17-20) and by Paul (I Cor. 11:23-26). It is equally clear that Jesus enjoined his followers to observe the ordinance until he comes again (Lk. 22:19; I Cor. 11:23-26). The practice of the early churches leaves little doubt that the disciples of Jesus understood the Lord's Supper to be a permanent ordinance (cf. Acts 2:42, 46; 20:7, I Cor. 10:16, 17; 11:17-34).

### The Participants
There is much discussion today as to who should partake of the Lord's Supper. Some have thought that the Bible is not clear on this matter, and it should be left up to the individual as to whether or not he should partake of it. However, the Bible is more definite on this question than some suppose.

It is clear, for instance, that only believers are entitled to partake of the Supper. The whole world is not invited to it. The very nature of the Supper as the communion of the body and blood of Christ indicates that the Lord's table is only for those who share in him (I Cor. 10:16). In the New Testament practice those who shared in the "breaking of bread" were those who "gladly received his word" and "continued stedfastly in the apostles' doctrine" (Acts 2:41-42).

But there is also an indication that the Lord's Supper is only for members of a local church. It is a local church ordinance. The administration of the ordinance is not given to an individual, or to the clergy. The responsibility for administering it was given to the church. Thus, the church was to observe it together as a corporate group and not privately (I Cor. 11:33). Furthermore, the church had a right to forbid certain people from partaking of the ordinance (I Cor. 5:11).

### Its Meaning
There has been much controversy among Christians through the centuries over the meaning of the Lord's Supper. The controversy has centered around the nature of the elements - the bread and the fruit of the vine. Some have thought that the bread and wine become the actual body and blood of Jesus when properly blessed. Others have taught that while the elements do not become the physical body and blood of Jesus, there is nevertheless a real spiritual presence of Jesus in the elements.

Baptists believe that the meaning of the ordinance is primarily summed up in the command of Christ, "This do in remembrance of me" (Lk. 22:19; I Cor. 11:24-25). It "is a symbolic act of obedience whereby members of the church, through partaking of the bread and fruit of the vine, memorialize the death of the Redeemer and anticipate His second coming" (**Baptist Faith and Message,** Art. VII).

Thus, the primary meaning of the Lord's Supper is that it is a symbolic memorial. It is a remembrance of two things. It is first and foremost a remembrance of the death of Jesus (I Cor. 11:25-26).

Both elements in the Supper point to his death - the bread his broken body (I Cor. 14:24) and the fruit of the vine his shed blood (I Cor. 14:25). But it is also a reminder that Jesus not only died but was raised from the dead and is coming again (I Cor. 14:26).

## 45. THE GOVERNMENT OF THE CHURCH

Does the New Testament teach a definite governmental form for a gospel church? Some do not think so. They maintain that as there are different forms in government in human societies, so there may be different forms of government in and among the Lord's churches. They suggest that any form of government which the Holy Spirit can use is proper and valid for the churches.

In the main, there are four types of governments which have been suggested and practiced by various Christian groups: (1) the monarchial, in which the ultimate authority lies in one man, the Roman Catholic Church; (2) the episcopal, in which the church is governed by a group or body of officers called bishops, such as the Episcopal and Methodist Churches; (3) the presbyterial, in which the local church is governed by elders, with higher courts or authority over them; and (4) the congregational, in which the seat of authority lies within the local church as a self governing body, such as Baptists.

Does it really make a difference which of these types of government is practiced by the Lord's churches? Baptists insist that it does. We feel that there is a definite governmental structure for the church laid down in the Scriptures, and is thus to be followed today.

The **Baptist Faith and Message** defines what Baptist believe the New Testament form of church government to be as follows: "The church is an autonomous body, operating through democratic processes under the Lordship of Jesus Christ. In such a congregation members are equally responsible" (Art. VI).

In this statement two ideas are present. First, a local church is an autonomous body. The term "autonomous" means self governing. This word is used to express the idea that a local church is free from any outside control. The local church has no person or organization above it except the Lord Jesus Christ himself.

The second idea in this statement is that the local church is governed by democratic processes. This means that the ultimate authority is vested in the members themselves and not in a person or board within the church. Of course there are elected officers with delegated authority, but this authority rests upon their relation to the congregation.

Now, upon what biblical facts do we base this understanding of chruch government? There are two:

First, the New Testament churches were organized according to this plan. The New Testament presents no church organization above the local church. It was the final court of appeal in settling differences between believers (Mt. 18:15-17). The local church was to discipline its own members (I Cor. 5:5); elect its own officers and representatives (Acts 6:3-5; Acts 14:23; Tit. 1:5); and had responsibility of maintaining true doctrine and practice (I Jn. 4:1, I Th. 5:21; Rev. 2:2).

Second, a democratic autonomous local church is also based upon certain other fundamental Christian teachings. One of these is the Lordship of Christ. Another is the doctrine of salvation by grace through faith and the priesthood of every believer. A third is the indwelling of the Holy Spirit in the life of every believer. All of these doctrines carry with them the idea of a democratic congregational form of church government.


## 46. THE MISSION AND WORK OF THE CHURCH

The mission of the church is a much discussed issue in Christian circles today. There are many voices suggesting that the church's mission needs to be redefined. Much of what the churches have been doing is totally irrelevant for today's world, it is said. That is, the times and conditions of the day should dictate what the mission of the church should be.

There is a sense in which the church should adapt to the needs of a changing world. However, the source of reference for determining the mission of Christ's churches must always be the Bible. We must never let the world describe or determine our mission for us.

The Bible itself prepares us to expect that much of what we are commissioned by our Lord to do will appear irrelevant to an unregenerate world. In Paul's day the preaching of the cross was foolishness to a perishing world (I Cor. 1: 18), and things have not changed much. It may grieve us that a large segment of society rejects our message as being outdated, but it should not surprise us.

Using the Bible as our source of reference we may sum up the mission of the church as having a three-fold function. This three-fold function relates the mission of the church to the world, to itself, and to God.

### Its Mission To The World

First, the church has a mission to the world. Here its primary mission is the proclamation of the gospel--that is, evangelism. The biblical evidence for this is manifold and plain. The primary purpose for which Jesus came into the world was to "seek and save that which is lost" (Lk. 19: 10). What is known as the Great Commission is repeated five times in the Scriptures, and the essential element in each is that of evangelism (Mt. 28: 19-20; Mk. 16:15; Lk. 24: 46-48; Jn. 20: 21; Acts 1: 8).

It is clear that the early churches understood the ministry of evangelism to be their primary mission to the world. They went from house to house teaching and preaching Jesus is the Christ (Acts 5: 42). The apostles made it clear that their primary mission was the ministry of the word (Acts 6: 4), which resulted in the number of disciples being multiplied (Acts 6: 7). When scattered abroad the disciples "went every where preaching the word" (Acts 8: 4).

## Mission to Itself

Second, the church has a mission toward itself. This mission is that of edification of one another. Edification means "to build up." It is very frequently used with reference to erecting a building. With reference to the church it refers to the building and developing the members in the life and faith (Eph. 4: 16; Jude 20; I Cor. 14: 26). The ultimate goal is that each member might attain the complete likeness of Christ (Eph. 4: 13-16).

There are several God-ordained means through which the church is to achieve its mission of edification. Ultimately, of course, it is the work of the Holy Spirit to bring us all to Christlikeness (Gal. 5: 22-23). However, the Spirit uses the special ministries of God-appointed leaders (Eph. 4: 11-12). Also every individual member has a responsibility or part to play in edifying the whole body. This is done through exhorting, encouraging, and comforting one another (I Thes. 5:11; Heb. 10:24-25), and through the exercise of the Spiritual gifts (I Cor. 12: 4-11).

## Mission Toward God

Finally, the church has a mission toward God. This mission is to glorify Him and His Son Jesus. This is really the ultimate goal of all the functions of the church, whether it is evangelism, edification, or whatever. No work of the church should be an end in itself, not even evangelism. The end of all the church does is to glorify the triune God. For to Him belongs the "glory in the church by Christ Jesus throughout all ages, world without end, Amen" (Eph. 3:21).

92

# Part IX

## ANGELS AND DEMONS

## 47. THE DOCTRINE OF ANGELS

The subject of angels is one of those doctrines which is quite frequently overlooked or ignored in doctrinal studies. Most Christians are aware that they are mentioned in the Bible, but little is known about them.

### Their Existence

Many people are inclined to dismiss the existence of angels as an outmoded belief impossible to hold in this scientific age. However, if the Bible is to be believed, there can be no doubt that angels do exist. Their existence is acknowledged throughout the Old Testament. From earliest times to the close of the Old Testament period, angels played a role in God's communication of Himself to man (cf. Gen. 19: 1; Psa. 91: 11; Dan. 3: 28). As far as the New Testament is concerned, the evidence is clear that Jesus and the apostles believed in and taught the existence of angels (Mt. 18: 10; Mk. 13: 32; 2 Thes. 1: 7; Jn. 1: 51; I Pe. 3:22).

### Their Nature

Several things may be concluded from the biblical references concerning the nature of angels:

First, they are created beings (Col. 1: 16). Just when they were created is not specifically stated in the Bible. There is some indication that they were created at the time God created the heavenly system. While their creation is not expressly mentioned in the Genesis account, it is strongly implied (cf. Gen. 2: 1; Ex. 20: 11). At any rate, their creation apparently took place before the creation of the earth for they rejoiced at the event (Job 38: 7).

Second, angels are spiritual beings (Psa. 104: 4; Heb. 1: 14). Although they are spiritual in nature, they frequently appeared to men in visible and human form (Gen. 19; Jdgs. 2: 1; 6: 11-22; Mt. 1:20; Lk. 1: 26; Jn. 20: 12). However, these material appearances were for the purposes of divine revelation and were only temporary.

Third, angels are supernatural creatures with great knowledge and power. They "excel in strength" (Psa. 103: 20) and are "greater in power and might" than man (2 Pe. 2: 11). One angel was able to destroy 185,000 Assyrian soldiers (Isa. 37: 36). Other similar feats are attributed to angels (cf. Gen. 19: 10-13; Rev. 20: 2, 10).

### Their Work

What do angels do? According to the biblical references their work is manifold and varied. They have a heavenly ministry which consists mainly of priestly service and worship. They praise God, celebrate the glory of His perfections, and keep His commandments (Isa. 6; Rev. 5: 11, 12; 8: 3,4).

They also have an earthly ministry which is related primarily to the children of God. They observe the walk of believers (I Cor. 4: 9; Eph. 3: 10); help them in distress (Heb. 1: 14; Acts 12: 7); fight for their final victory (Dan. 12: 1; Rev. 12: 7-9); cheer and strengthen them in time of trials (I Kgs. 19: 5-8; Mt. 4: 4:11); and reveal the mind and will of God to them (Deut. 32: 2; Acts 7: 59; Heb. 2: 2).

## A Warning

As a final word, a warning must be given. Angels are not gods. They are creatures and servants of God, but not themselves gods. Accordingly, they are not to be worshipped nor venerated. Such a practice is forbidden and strongly rebuked throughout the Bible (Col. 2: 18; Rev. 19: 10).


## 48. THE DOCTRINE OF SATAN

The doctrine of Satan is one of those biblical doctrines which has been the subject of much ridicule in modern times. While there seems to be a renewed interest in the subject, it is probably true that the great majority of people feel that Satan is only the figment of our imaginations. The existence of a real devil surely cannot be taken seriously by the twentieth-century man.

### A Real Personality

In light of the widespread doubt as to the existence of Satan, it is necessary to state that the Bible very clearly and positively teaches that the devil is a real person. Throughout the Bible the attributes and qualities of personality are ascribed to him. He is called a murderer and a liar (Jn. 8:44), and it is said that he commits sin (I Jn. 3:8). All of these are elements of a real person.

It is certain that Jesus believed in and taught the existence of a personal devil. No one can read the story of the temptations without seeing this Mt. 4:1-11). Throughout His teachings Jesus makes reference to Satan and his work, and he always refers to him in personal terms (cf. Mt. 13:19, 39; 25:41; Lk. 11:21; Jn. 14:30).

### His Character and Work

The character of Satan is expressed in the names and titles given to him in the Bible. The two terms most frequently used to refer to this evil personality are "satan" and "devil." The title "Satan" means "adversary," someone who takes a stand against another. In this case, Satan is one who opposes God and His people. The term "devil" means "slanderer." Thus the essential character of Satan is the opposite of God. He is the enemy of God and His followers, and his intent is set on malicious evil against both. For this reason he is appropriately called the "wicked one" (Mt. 13:19; I Jn. 2:14).

Satan's work is in keeping with his essential nature. All his actions are designed primarily to oppose or thwart the purposes of God. He incites men to evil (Lk. 22:3; Acts 5:3). He hinders the activity of God's messengers (I Th. 2:18). He causes false beliefs to arise (I. Tim. 5:15; cf. Gal. 5:8). He tempts men to disobey God (Gen. 3:1-6; Mt. 4:1-11). He inspires persecution against believers (I Pe. 5:8; Rev. 2:13). He blinds the minds of the lost to the gospel and causes them to believe a lie (2 Cor. 4:4; 2 Thes. 2:8-11).

### His Position and Power

There are two erroneous views concerning the power of Satan. Some attribute to him too much power, making him almost equal to God. Others would deny him any power at all. The Bible rejects both of these extremes.

The Bible, on the one hand, attributes to Satan supernatural power. He has the power to resist one of the chief angels (Dan. 10:12-13; Jude 8,9). He is called the "prince of this world" (Jn. 14:30), "the prince of the power of the air" (Eph. 2:2), and "the god of this world" (2 Cor. 4:4). All these terms surely intend to convey the idea that Satan has been endowed with great power, so much so that the "whole world lieth in the wicked one" (I Jn. 5:19, R.V.).

On the other hand, the Bible plainly recognizes that Satan's power is limited. One sometimes gets the impression from the current discussions on the subject of Satan that his power is such that we are hopelessly held in his clutches. Thank God, this is not true (cf. Col. 2:15; Ja. 4:7; Lk. 10:18-19). He is not God, and his power and authority is thus limited by the sovereign power and authority of God (Job 1:12, 2:6; Jd. 9). Thus the Christian can resist the devil (Ja. 4:7), and stand against him (Eph. 6:11).

## 49. DEMONOLOGY

Time was when you would rarely hear the subject of demons mentioned or discussed in Christian circles. This is no longer true today. There is presently a very lively interest in the subject. In fact, there seems to be a preoccupation with the whole realm of the spirit world, especially with demonology. More than ever before in modern times Christians need to be informed concerning the biblical teaching about demons.

## Their Existence

Many feel that there is no such thing as demons, that they are merely the creation of superstition and imagination. However, the New Testament presents unrefutable evidence for the existence of demons. The Gospels relate a mighty outburst of demon activity during the public ministry of Jesus. They opposed the mission of Christ (Mt. 4: 1-10; Mk. 5: 1-10). The casting out of demons was one of the most frequently performed miracles of Jesus (Mt. 15:22,28), and he gave his disciples authority to do the same (Mt. 10: 1). Their existence is also witnessed in the rest of the New Testament (cf. Ja. 2: 19; Eph. 6: 10-20; I Tim. 4: 1; Rev. 9: 11; 16: 14).

## Their Nature

The New Testament gives us a great deal of information concerning the nature of demons. We know that they are real personalities. They are capable of intelligent, voluntary actions, such as thinking, speaking, and acting (Mk. 5: 10; Lk. 4: 34; Acts 19: 15-16). We know also that they are spiritual beings (Mt. 8: 16; Lk. 10: 17, 20; Eph. 6: 12). They are beings with great power (cf. 2 Pe. 2: 11; Mt. 12: 29; Eph. 6: 10ff.). Demons are "unclean" spirits, which means they are depraved and wicked in their nature (Mt. 10:1; Mk. 1:27; Lk. 4:36; Acts 8:7).

## Their Work

The work of demons is essentially the same as that of Satan. Their main occupation is that of opposing the will and purposes of God. In this work, people often become the victims of their evil deeds. They oppress, influence, and subject the minds of men. Demons had control of the mind of the maniac of Gadara, and only after they had been expelled was he in his "right mind" (Mk. 5:15). They also oppress the body and hinder man's general well being (Mt. 9: 32, 33; 12: 33; Lk. 13: 11-17). They use men to hinder the work of God (cf. Acts 16: 16-18; 19: 11-20).

## Demon Activity Today

There can be no doubt concerning the existence and activity of demons in New Testament times. But what about the activity of demons today? As far as the biblical record is concerned there is nothing in it which would cause us to believe that demon activity ceased after the New Testament age. In fact, the Bible indicates the opposite. There is indication that demon activity will increase in the last days (cf. I Tim. 4: 1; Rev. 9: 1-21).

## Christ's Authority Over Demons

With all the talk about demons today, one might get the impression that man is a helpless victim of demons. Not so! God is still sovereign and in perfect control of the universe. The healthy Christian has nothing to fear from demons, for in Christ our victory is complete. This does not mean that believers will never be confronted with demonic power. Indeed, they will. But ours is the victory in the Lord (Eph. 6: 10ff.).

# Part X

# THE DOCTRINE OF LAST THINGS

# 50. INTRODUCTION

These doctrinal studies have brought us finally to the doctrine of last things. This area of Christian doctrine is called eschatology. It comes from the Greek word **eschaton,** which means "last" or "end." Hence, eschatology is a study of last things.

The **Baptist Faith and Message** contains the following article of "Last Things":

"God, in His own time and His own way, will bring the world to its appropriate end. According to His promise, Jesus Christ will return personally and visibly in glory to the earth; the dead will be raised; and Christ will judge all men in righteousness. The unrighteous will be consigned to Hell, the place of everlasting punishment. The righteous in their resurrected, glorified bodies will receive their reward and will dwell forever in Heaven with the Lord." (Art. X)

One can see from this statement on last things that the doctrine of eschatology deals with a number of subjects. It deals with such matters as death and what happens afterwards, the second coming of Christ, the resurrection, the question of the millennium, the judgment, and the final destinies of both the saved and the lost-- heaven and hell.

In some circles the doctrine of last things is minimized. It is thought that these matters are too "other worldly" to be taken seriously by modern man. The great emphasis is social action. Life in the present is the all important thing. The watchword is the now. The future is of no concern; it will take care of itself. Eschatology is berated as a "pie in the sky by and by" theology.

To those who take the Bible seriously the doctrine of last things is of importance. It is important because it is a part of our salvation. Salvation, to be sure, is a present deliverance from guilt and bondage of sin. However, our salvation is not complete until God consummates it in the future. The Bible has a great deal to say about this consummation. To neglect eschatology or berate it is to admit that a great part of the Bible is of no consequence.

Fortunately, there is a revival of interest in eschatology today. Much is being written on the subject today. Some of the best selling religious books deal with some aspect of last things. This is a welcome return to a significant biblical doctrine.

Certain aspects of eschatology have been the source of much disagreement among biblical interpreters. This is especially true in the area of millennial studies. Most Baptists have never made the millennial question a test of fellowship. Different views are held within our fellowship.

Disagreement over some aspects of last things does not mean,

100

however, that the Bible is unclear on all matters dealing with eschatology. Nor does it mean that there is no agreement among Baptists on other aspects of last things. While in this series on last things we will not hesitate to deal with the controversial, we will emphasize those things we have in common.


## 51. DEATH AND THE INTERMEDIATE STATE

Despite the fact that death is an unpleasant subject, we can hardly avoid thinking about it some time or other. What is death? What happens after death? Is there a life of conscious existence afterward? These are questions quite frequently asked of clergymen.

In the doctrine of eschatology or last things these questions are some of the first issues we face. In looking at what the Bible teaches about these matters we will look first at what it has to say about death, then a word about the intermediate state.

### Death
First, the Bible teaches that death is real. It is the common lot of all men (Heb. 9:27). All who have lived on earth have died, with only two notable exceptions--Enoch and Elijah (Heb. 11:5; 2 Kgs. 2: 11). Furthermore, all who are now living on earth will die, unless, of course, the Lord comes in this generation.

Second, the Bible teaches that physical death is a separation of soul and body. This is often denied by contemporary theologians. But the Bible is clear enough on this matter. Death is described as "giving up the spirit" (Mt. 27: 50). The Old Testament states that at death the body returns to dust and "the spirit returneth unto God who gave it" (Ecc. 12: 7).

In addition, Paul speaks of death as a departure (Phi. 1: 23; 2 Tim. 4: 6). The picture here is of a ship putting out to sea for another shore. The clear implication is that while the body is laid to rest or asleep (Acts 7: 60; I Thes. 4: 13), the spirit takes its departure into another world.

Third, the New Testament teaches that Christ has overcome the evil power of death. Death for the believer is thus not to be feared. It is rather to be looked upon as an entrance into a more glorious and fuller life. Death has been abolished for the believer (II Tim. 1: 10). It no longer has any sting (I Cor. 15: 54-57). It cannot separate us from the love of God (Rom. 8: 38). It is simply a falling asleep (Jn. 11: 11; I Thes. 4: 13). Death is even considered an asset rather than a liability (I Cor. 3: 21-22; Phil. 1:23).

## The Intermediate State

The place and condition of the dead between death and the resurrection is called the intermediate state. It deals with the question, Where does one go when he dies?

Two truths revealed in the Scriptures about the state of the dead need to be emphasized:

First, it is clear that the righteous are in a state of conscious existence with the Lord (Phil. 1: 23; II Cor. 5: 8). That this is a state of conscious existence is strongly implied in the story of Jesus about the rich man and Lazarus (cf. Lk. 16: 22, 24). Paul's desire to depart and to be with the Lord can hardly be explained if he did not think that he would have a conscious existence after he departed (Phil. 1: 23).

Second, it is clear that the unrighteous have a state of conscious existence apart from God. This is clearly taught in the story of Jesus about the rich man and Lazarus (Lk. 16: 19-31). In this story there are repeated references to feelings and consciousness. He saw (v. 23); he spake (v. 24); he felt (v. 23, 24); he remembered (v. 25), and he was conscious of what was going on in earth (v. 27-28). In addition Peter plainly states that God is keeping "the unrighteous under punishment unto the day of judgment" (II Pe. 2: 8; ASV).

## 52. THE SECOND COMING OF CHRIST

The second coming of Christ is one of the most prominent doctrines in the New Testament. It is unfortunate that certain controversies have caused many to neglect this great New Testament truth. There are some signs of a revived interest in this coming event, but there still are many who shy away from it. Consequently, many Christians are uninformed about even the essential biblical facts concerning the doctrine. We need to remember that it was Paul's desire that believers not be "ignorant" of this matter (I Thess. 4: 13).

A comprehensive view of the coming of the Lord has many facets to it. As we have already indicated, there are some differences over the particulars. However, there is common agreement among evangelical Christians concerning most of the essentials. The New Testament is so plain on these matters that no one can deny them without discrediting the Scriptures. These all-important essentials which should be firmly held regardless of any differences concerning details consists of the following:

## The Fact

First, the New Testament is clear concerning the fact of Christ's coming. There can be no possible doubt that the Bible teaches that Jesus is coming. The scriptural references to this event are so numerous that we cannot begin to list them all in this study. It is referred to some three hundred times in the New Testament alone (an average of one in every fifteen verses). There are at least eight different writers of the New Testament, and every one, without exception, mentions the coming of the Lord (cf. Mt. 24: 30; Mk. 13: 26; Lk. 17: 24; Jn. 14: 3; I Thes. 4: 16; Ja. 5: 7; I Pe. 5: 4; Jd. 14).

## The Manner

Second, the New Testament is clear concerning the manner of Christ's coming. His coming will be personal (Acts 1: 11), bodily (Acts 1: 11), and visible (Rev. 1: 7).

Attempts have been made to spiritualize the coming of the Lord in one way or another. Some have taught that His promise to return was fulfilled with the descent of the Spirit at Pentecost. Others have sought to explain it as the death of the believer. Some have connected it with the destruction of Jerusalem in 70 A.D. Still others simply understand it to be His continuing presence in the world.

None of these ideas is adequate to explain the plain promises in the New Testament. The New Testament plainly refers to a literal personal return of Christ sometime in the future. It will be an actual event as real as His first coming.

## The Purpose

Third, the New Testament has some clear statements on the purpose of His coming. He is coming to be personally glorified as Lord and King (II Thes. 1: 10), to raise the dead (I Thes. 4: 16), to reward the believers (Rev. 22: 12), to judge the unbelieving (II Thes. 1: 8), to completely put down evil (I Cor. 15: 23-28), and to bring in His glorious kingdom (Rev. 20: 1-5).

## The Time

Fourth, the New Testament is quite definite as to the time of our Lord's return. No one can know the exact time. It is hidden in the undisclosed will of God (Mt. 24: 36-42). Our Lord warns us that He may come at any time (Mt. 25: 13), that it will be sudden and unannounced (I Thes. 5: 3), and that we are always to be ready (Mt. 24: 44).

## 53. THE RESURRECTION

The resurrection from the dead is one of the great affirmations of the Christian faith. The Bible teaches that when a Christian dies, his spirit goes to be with the Lord, but his body returns to dust. But that is not the end of it. It will be raised again, a redeemed body, suited for the redeemed spirit.

The doctrine of the resurrection has always raised questions in peoples' minds. In Paul's day they were asking, "How are the dead raised? And with what manner of body do they come?" (I Cor. 15: 35). People are asking these same questions today. Some are skeptical and unbelieving like the Saduccees (Mt. 22: 23-28). Others simply do not know but are sincerely interested in what the Bible has to say about the subject.

### The Nature

The New testament teaches us that the resurrection will be a literal bodily resurrection. This is seen in the fact that the believer is to view the nature of his own resurrection body as identical with that of Christ's glorified body (Phil. 3: 21; I Cor. 15: 49; I Jn. 3: 2). Christ's resurrection body was a real body (Lk. 24: 39); recognizable (Lk. 24: 31), and unlimited by space (Jn. 20: 19). The believer's body thus will have similar features.

In I Cor. 15 Paul gives us a little more detail as to the nature of the believer's body. There are two points especially which may be stressed from this passage. First, the resurrection body will have a definite connection with the old body. The new body will have a similar connection with the old body as a plant has to a seed (I Cor. 15: 37). It will be recognizable as that which was planted.

Second, there will be a glorious change in the resurrection body. It will not be simply the old body. Paul describes that change in I Cor. 15: 42-49. The new body will be incorruptible, glorious, powerful, and spiritual.

### The Time

There is no question as to when the believers will be raised. It will be when Jesus comes again (I Cor. 15: 23; I Thes. 4: 16). However, the resurrection of the unbeliever is not mentioned in connection with this event. Because of this there are two views as to when unbelievers will be raised.

Some believe that believers and unbelievers will be raised at the same time. This is known as the general resurrection. Others believe that there will be a period of time between the resurrection of believers and unbelievers--namely, the millennial reign of Christ.

It seems to this writer that the latter view best explains all the biblical facts. The Bible seems to distinguish between the resurrection of the just and the unjust (Dan. 12:2; Jn. 5:28-29)), and there is a clear reference to two resurrections with a time period in between (Rev. 20: 4-6).

While equally devout Baptist people may differ in their views as to whether there is one or two resurrections, all agree that both the righteous and the wicked will be raised, one to everlasting life, the other to judgment and everlasting hell.

### The Basis
How do we know these things? The assurance of our resurrection is based upon the resurrection of Christ. Paul argues that since Christ has been raised from the dead, so will the believer (I Cor. 15: 12-19). If there is no resurrection for the believer, then Christ has not been raised (I Cor. 15: 13). Unthinkable!

## 54. THE MILLENNIUM

Any discussion of last things must eventually come to the much debated question of the millennium. The term itself is made up of two Latin words--**mille,** a thousand, and **annus,** a year--meaning a thousand years. In Christian doctrine it refers to the thousand years reign of Christ mentioned in Rev. 20: 1-10.

The nature of the Book of Revelation and the consequent difficulties encountered in interpreting Rev. 20: 1-10 have resulted in differing views concerning the millennium. Basically there are three main schools of thought--postmillennialism, premillennialism, and amillennialism. Here we can give only a brief outline of these views.

### Postmillennialism
Postmillennialism interprets the thousand years in Rev. 20: 1-10 figuratively. According to this view the great majority of the world will be converted to Christ through the preaching of the gospel. This will result in a period of universal peace, righteousness, and justice. Thus the millennium stands for an indefinite long period of time in which there will be a "golden age" of spiritual and moral prosperity. At the close of this "golden age" Christ will come, the dead, both the righteous and wicked, will be raised, and the judgment will follow.

### Amillennialism
Amillennialism means no millennium. Like postmillennialism this school of thought interprets Rev. 20: 1-10 symbolically and

spiritually, but it rejects the notion of an earthly millennium altogether--whether spiritual or material. This view believes that the Bible teaches that good and evil will continue side by side until the end of time. Christ may come at any time. When He does the dead will be raised and there will be a final judgment at which the saved and lost will be separated. Then eternity begins.

### Premillennialism

The premillennialists insist that the thousand years in Rev. 20: 1-10 refer to a literal reign of Christ on earth. This reign will be established when Christ comes again.

Most premillennialists--not all--believe that the Bible teaches that there will be two phases to the Second Coming of Christ. First, there will be a coming for His saints. This is called the "rapture" of the church (I Thes. 4: 15-17). At this time the dead in Christ will be raised, living Christians will be changed, and together they will be caught up in the clouds to meet the Lord. Following this, and preceding the millennium, there will be a period of tribulation on the earth, during which time the Jews will be converted and become messengers of the gospel.

Second, there will be a coming with His saints. At the close of the tribulation period Christ will return to the earth with His saints for a thousand years. This is the millennium. At the close of this period Satan will be loosed but quickly subdued again. The wicked will be raised from the dead and judged at the Great White Throne Judgment.

### Personal Conclusion

Devout Christians have disagreed through the ages over the millennium. Whatever position one takes he should be careful to have the right attitude toward those who differ. Premillennialists have frequently charged the other two views with liberalism and accused those who hold them of being Bible deniers. On the other hand the other two views have often charged premillennialists with ignorance and fanaticism.

With due respect to the other views, this writer holds to the premillennial view. To be sure, the main issue is the fact that Christ is coming. However, Rev. 20: 1-10 is in the Bible, as are other passages dealing with a "golden age" (cf. Isa. 2: 1-5; 11: 1-9), and must be interpreted. To me the premillennial view best fits all the biblical facts.

## 55. THE FINAL JUDGMENT

The idea of a judgment day to come is a prominent idea in the Bible. While modern men often have difficulty with the concept of a universal judgment, the writers of the Bible considered it to be a fact beyond dispute. It inevitably arises from the nature of God as righteous. As righteous God must punish sin and reward righteousness.

Since the Bible has so much to say about a final judgment, we can select only a few points to emphasize here.

### The Judge

In a vision of the final judgment John saw a "great white throne, and him that sat upon it" (Rev. 20: 11). He does not identify the person on the throne, but other scriptural references leave little doubt as to his identity. The judge will be none other than Jesus Himself (cf. Jn. 5: 22, 27; Acts 17: 31; 2 Thes. 4: 1).

This is an awesome thought. Throughout the New Testament Jesus appears as our Saviour. As such, it is possible for people to pass Him by, to ignore Him, even to deny His very existence. But when He appears as Judge there will be no ignoring Him. Then His presence and authority will be inescapable (2 Thes. 1: 7f; 2 Pet. 3: 10; Jude 14f.).

### The Scope

Two things are emphasized in the Bible concerning the scope of the judgment. First, it will be universal. None shall escape it. Both the living and the dead will be there (2 Tim. 4:1; I Pet. 4:5). The important, the rich, and the powerful will not be able to avoid it (Rev. 20: 12). The insignificant, the poor, and the weak will be involved (Rev. 20: 12). All people, without any exceptions, must stand before the judgment bar of God. This includes believers as well as unbelievers.

In this respect it should be pointed out that some interpreters, of whom this writer is one, believe there is a difference between the judgment of believers and the judgment of unbelievers. The judgment of believers is called the Judgment Seat of Christ (Rom. 14: 10; II Cor. 5: 10). The judgment of unbelievers is the Great White Throne Judgment (Rev. 20: 11-15). Nevertheless, even though there is a difference in the judgments of believers and unbelievers, it remains true that believers will also have to face a type of judgment. So, all will be judged.

A second factor in the scope of the judgment is that it will be complete. The judgment will include all things. Nothing can be kept hid (Rom. 2: 16). It will include thoughts (I Cor. 4: 5), words (Mt.

12: 36), and deeds (Rev. 20: 13). The scope of the judgment is thus far-reaching and all-inclusive.

### The Manner
Christ will judge the world in righteousness (Acts 17: 31). This means that the judgment will be absolutely fair. There will be no mistakes, no miscarriages of justice. It also means that there will be no respecter of persons. A person's status or position here on earth will mean nothing at the judgment.

Injustices are some of the most frustrating facts of life here on earth. Only God knows how many miscarriages of justice are made, knowingly and unknowingly, in the judgment halls of men. Thank the Lord, none of this will be a part of His judgment.

### The Results
There is no uncertainty in the Bible concerning the outcome of the judgment. Its purpose is not to decide one's destiny. That is decided here and now. All without Christ, those whose names are not in the Lamb's Book of Life, will be eternally condemned. This is as certain as the judgment itself (cf. Jn. 3:18; Rev. 20: 14-15; 21: 8).

But the believer has nothing to fear. His sins have already been judged (Jn. 3: 18; 5: 24; Rom. 8:1). Christ's redemptive work has already acquitted the beliver, and when he stands before God    he will only hear, "NOT GUILTY."


## 56. THE DOCTRINE OF HELL

Probably no doctrine of the Christian faith is more universally rejected than the doctrine of hell. One of the most appealing ideas in theological circles is that of universalism--the belief that ultimately everyone will be  saved. It seems almost impossible for modern man to think in terms of a future punishment for humanity.

Despite the widespread revolt against the notion of hell, Christians must be true to the teaching of Scripture. Christians do not first inquire as to what modern man thinks about a certain matter and then seek to conform biblical teaching to that opinion. We ask first, "What saith the Scriptures?" On the subject of hell, the answer is plain and certain.

### A Real Place
Hell is a real place. It is not merely a state of mind nor is it simply the troubles a person might experience here on earth. Neither is it to be understood as some kind of undefinable spiritual separation from

God. It is a real place of conscious existence in the "other world." It is a place where bodies will be as well as souls (Mt. 10:28), and these bodies will experience the physical sensations of seeing, speaking, hearing, and feeling (cf. Lk. 16:23,24).

### A Place of Punishment
Hell is a place of punishment. This idea is particularly repulsive to the modern mind. It is, nevertheless, unmistakably taught in the Bible (2 Thes. 1: 9; Mt. 25: 46). Even the very descriptions of hell themselves demonstrate that it is a place of punishment. It is represented as a prison (I Pe. 3: 19-20; 2 Pe. 2:4), a state of darkness (Mt. 8: 12, Jd. 13), a place of fire (Mt. 5:22), and a place where the worm never dies (Mk. 9: 44, 46, 48), and where there will be weeping and gnashing of teeth (Mt. 13: 42, 50).

We are told something about the nature of the punishment in hell. It will be of two kinds. There will be a punishment in the form of a loss. The loss consists of a deprivation of all good things--a separation from God and His Son Jesus Christ, the chiefest of good (Mt. 7: 23; 25: 41; 2 Thes. 1: 9), from the company of the righteous and the holy angels (Psa. 1: 5; Lk. 16: 26), and from the kingdom of God and all that means (Mt. 8: 11-12; Jn. 3: 5).

But the punishment consists also of a positive infliction of suffering. There will be "indignation and wrath, tribulation and anguish, upon every soul of man that doeth evil" (Rom. 2: 8-9). There will be torments of flames of fire (Lk. 16: 24). The believer should be thankful that he will never know the full meaning of these terms.

### An Eternal State
While it is widely denied, there can be no doubt that the Bible represents hell as eternal. The adjective "eternal" or "everlasting" is frequently used in describing hell and the future punishment of the wicked (Mt. 18 :8; 25:41,46; 2 Thes. 1:9; Heb. 6:2; Jd. 6). This is the same adjective used to describe the everlasting life given to the believer. Thus, the punishment meted out to the unbeliever will last as long as the life given to the believer.


There are some who feel the idea of an eternal hell is inconsistent with the love of God. If one is tempted to accept this criticism, he should keep in mind that Jesus, the one who taught and demonstrated the love of God more than any other, has the most forceful statements about hell. Note the number of references to the teachings of Jesus throughout this study. And there are plenty more.

## 57. THE DOCTRINE OF HEAVEN

Heaven is the final abode of the saints. While the term may be used to describe the dwelling place of the righteous during the intermediate state (see Study Number 51), the term more properly denotes the eternal state of the righteous after the resurrection, the millennium, and the judgment.

### A Real Place

Heaven is a real place. In the Scriptures it is called a place (Jn. 14: 2), a country (Heb. 11: 14-16), a city (Heb. 11: 10, 16; 12: 22; 13: 14; Rev. 21: 10-27), and a house or mansion (Jn. 14: 2-3). Some of these expressions are no doubt figurative, but they stand for something. The Bible knows nothing of a non-material, spaceless, ethereal kind of abode in eternity. Heaven is more than a condition of the soul, more than a state of mind, more than mere thoughts and ideas. It is a dwelling place consisting of material reality.

In addition to the biblical descriptions of heaven, there are two other biblical truths of the Christian faith which demand that heaven be a real place. The first is the bodily resurrection and ascension of Christ, and the other is the bodily resurrection of the believers. The nature of heaven must correspond to these two facts. It is inconsistent, on the one hand, to believe in the bodily resurrection of flesh and bones with the capacity to eat and drink (cf. Lk. 24: 39-43; Acts 10: 41), and, on the other hand, to think of heaven as only symbolic and allegorical.

### A Glorious Life

What kind of life will we have in heaven? Many things could be said at this point, but we can only mention a few selected statements.

First, it will be a life of individual perfection. We will have new, perfect bodies (I Cor. 15: 42-58); our minds will be renewed (I Cor. 13: 12); we will have moral perfection for sin will be completely abolished from our nature and practice (I Jn. 3: 2; Eph. 5: 27; Rev. 21: 27). Imperfection is such a part of our experience now that it is almost impossible for us to conceive what this life will be like.

Second, it will be a life of harmonious social relations. People from all walks of life and from all races and nations will be in heaven (Rev. 7:9), and yet there will be no quarrels, disagreements, crimes, nor wars to mar the fellowship. In heaven there will be no fear nor mistrust of one another (Rev. 21: 24-27).

Third, it will be a life free from all natural evils. The body will no longer be subject to sickness, decay, hunger, pain, weariness, nor

110

death (I Cor. 15: 53; Rev. 7: 16; 21: 4). The ravages of nature will no longer be a threat for there will be a new heaven and a new earth with these taken away (Rom. 8: 18-22; Rev. 21: 1).

Finally, we know that heaven will be a life of unbroken fellowship with God. Our relations with God are so often hindered here. Sin often hides his face from us, and our limited understanding causes us to look through a glass darkly. But then we shall see Him face to face and behold Him in all His beauty (cf. Isa. 33: 7; Mt. 5: 8; Rev. 22: 4; I Jn. 3: 2). This will undoubtedly be the chiefest of joys in heaven, the bliss of all bliss. Oh, happy day!

### An Eternal State

It is sometimes said here, "All good things have to end some-time." This is not true of heaven. Heaven is the eternal state of the righteous. There will be no end to it. There will be no danger of ever falling from that blessed state, nor having it taken away from us. It is a world without end. Amen!